Northern Lights
The Story of Minnesota's Past

Northern Lights
The Story of Minnesota's Past

Rhoda R. Gilman

Minnesota Historical Society Press

St. Paul

1989

Copy and production editor: Ellen B. Green
Pilot design: Monica Little
Final design and layout: Thomas McGregor
Typesetting and keyline: Northwestern Printcrafters, Inc.
Printing: Viking Press, Inc.

10 9 8 7 6 5 4 3 2

Book ISBN: 0-87351-241-3   Set ISBN: 0-87351-243-X

Manufactured in the United States of America

Northern Lights
The Story of Minnesota's Past

Contents

Preface

This narrative of Minnesota history is part of a comprehensive curriculum intended for students in grades 5 through 7. Complementing it is a book of participatory activities that build the skills needed for historical thinking and introduce students to the sources from which historians construct a view of the past. Supplementing both books is a guide for teachers.

The *Northern Lights* curriculum was planned, researched, and written by staff members of the Minnesota Historical Society, drawing upon a wealth of resources collected over its 140-year life. It is written for students who live in a pluralistic society increasingly influenced by developing technology and by human impact on the natural environment. In no way should it be regarded as "official" history. It is the product of individual authors, and like all history, it carries assumptions and viewpoints.

We hope it represents fairly the men, women, and children of all groups and cultures who have been part of Minnesota's past. And we hope that in touching on a few of their personal stories it conveys to students some sense of the dreams, sorrows, conflicts, and complexities of the human journey. Where the words of individuals are quoted, we have sometimes shortened or simplified them for the benefit of young readers, but in all cases we have tried hard to keep the original meaning and feeling.

Work on the curriculum started early in 1983, and the list of all those who have aided us over the years of its development would run to several pages. Scholars and education specialists have been generous with their advice and critiques; teachers from all over the state have helped in reviewing and piloting the materials; members of minority groups have shared their recollections and viewpoints; citizens of the communities described in the first four chapters gave freely of their time, knowledge, and materials; state legislators listened with sympathy and support to our plea for funding of the pilot program; and the final product was made possible by a grant and loan from the Blandin Foundation of Grand Rapids, Minnesota.

Finally, recognition should go to staff members of the Minnesota Historical Society, many of whom went out of their way to give loyal support and cooperation to a project that at times seemed endless. Those directly responsible for *Northern Lights* have been Rhoda R. Gilman, author of *The Story of Minnesota's Past,* Stephen Sandell, author of *Going to the Sources,* Deborah Swanson and David Wiggins, research assistants, and Maureen Otwell, teacher education specialist. Ellen Green of E. B. Green Editorial served as editor and production coordinator; Monica Little of Little & Company and Thomas McGregor of McGregor Design were the designers. Photos by Thomas Bremer enliven both books.

Unit I
A Place of Many Faces

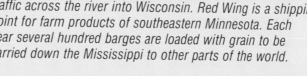

Chapter 1
Red Wing: A River Town

The Way the Waters Run

Looking at a map of North America you will see that Minnesota is a little to the north and east of the center. Close by are the Great Lakes. The finger of Lake Superior's western tip points to the city of Duluth. Above the northwest corner, like a feather in Minnesota's hat, is Lake Winnipeg. The long, wavy line of the Mississippi River starts in Minnesota and runs south a thousand miles or more to the Gulf of Mexico.

Minnesota seems flat. It has no towering mountains. Yet it is at the top of a hill. From this hill, water runs down in three directions. Some of it pours east through the Great Lakes to the Atlantic Ocean. The northwestern corner of the state slopes toward Lake Winnipeg. From there water flows north to Hudson Bay. But most of Minnesota is tipped southward, and most of its water pours into the great channel of the Mississippi.

Beginning as a small stream among the swamps and lakes of northern Minnesota, the Mississippi winds toward the southeastern part of the state. In the Twin Cities area, it pours over a large waterfall and is joined by two other important rivers—the Minnesota and the St. Croix. At the mouth of the St. Croix, the Mississippi becomes the border between Minnesota and Wisconsin.

In this 1986 photograph of the Mississippi River at Red Wing, Barn Bluff rises behind the grain storage buildings along the riverfront. The Hiawatha Bridge, opened in 1960, carries traffic across the river into Wisconsin. Red Wing is a shipping point for farm products of southeastern Minnesota. Each year several hundred barges are loaded with grain to be carried down the Mississippi to other parts of the world.

Old Man River

Minnesota's streams and rivers flow three ways. The lines dividing the state are called watersheds.

The Mississippi has a special meaning to Americans. Its name comes from an Ojibway (Chippewa) Indian word that is usually translated "Father of Waters." It is one of the world's largest rivers. Until the building of railroads, hundreds of paddle-wheeled steamboats, along with rafts and flatboats, linked the pioneer farms of the Midwest with the ocean port of New Orleans. The Mississippi carried lumber, wheat, corn products, furs, and hides from the heart of North America to the markets of the world. It was the country's busiest highway. Songs and sayings, plays and stories about it are part of our nation's tradition.

Towns and cities that grew up beside the Mississippi in the 1800s had a special character. Their people knew the tales, dangers, and excitement of steamboating and rafting on the great river. Travelers from distant places often passed through. So did the first news of national events. Steamboats brought crowds of immigrants and carried away loads of grain and other farm products.

One of these river towns was Red Wing. It was founded during a land rush in the early 1850s. Treaties with the Dakota (Sioux) Indians had given all of southern Minnesota to the United States, and pioneer farmers poured into the rolling prairie country west of the Mississippi. Many of those who came by steamboat got off at Red Wing.

They found that wheat grew well in the fertile new soil. With luck, a settler could pay for the land by raising one crop. The rich uplands of Goodhue County west of Red Wing filled with farms in the 1860s. For a

These paddle-wheeled steamboats were painted by Ferdinand Reichardt in 1857. They are on the Mississippi, a few miles below Red Wing.

while they produced more wheat than any other county in the nation. Without railroads, farmers had to haul their grain in wagons to river towns. There it was stored until it could be loaded on steamboats. Red Wing boomed. At one time its warehouses could hold a million bushels of grain.

In 1873 Red Wing led the whole country in the amount of wheat sold by farmers. But the bonanza soon ended. Railroads were built through southeastern Minnesota, and farmers began taking their grain to inland towns. Immigrants, too, traveled by train to the places they wanted to settle. The great days of the Mississippi were over.

At the Foot of Barn Bluff

Today most of Red Wing's visitors arrive by car. Driving from the north on U.S. Highway 61, you follow the Cannon River to where it enters the Mississippi from the west. There the road goes down a long hill. As you draw near the Mississippi, you can see the Wisconsin shore in the distance. The valley is more than three miles wide. Steep bluffs rise at its edges. From the air they look like the banks of a huge river, which is exactly what they once were.

Ten thousand years ago the valley was filled with a flood of water from melting ice. In the midst of the torrent was an island. With the water gone, the island has become a hill that is Red Wing's best-known landmark. It stands out from the Minnesota bluffs, and the Mississippi flows in a wide curve around it. Early travelers thought its steep sides and round top looked like a barn, so they called it Barn Bluff.

A tugboat pushes a barge down the river toward Red Wing. Freight carriers like this one now share the Mississippi with pleasure boats.

If you climb to the top of Barn Bluff, you can see Red Wing spread along the riverbank below. Close to the shore runs the railroad, with tall grain storage buildings on both sides. Next, also following the river, is U.S. 61. In town it becomes Main Street. The cross streets end at bluffs or disappear into narrow valleys between them. At the center of town is an open, grassy square with churches and public buildings around it. You might see the same kind of square in many New England towns. It tells you where the people who built Red Wing came from.

Just at your feet is the brown current of the Mississippi. A high bridge carries U.S. 63 across the river into Wisconsin. On the water a tugboat may be pushing a string of barges. To make the river safer for these heavy cargo carriers, the U.S. government has built a series of dams and deepened the channel. So in the last 50 years the Mississippi has again become an important highway for freight like coal and grain.

As you look upstream, the wall of bluffs on each side of the valley disappears in the distance. Between the hills the river seems to get lost in flat, wooded land crisscrossed by channels and lakes. About four miles away, two gray towers like the humps of a camel rise above the treetops. They belong to the Prairie Island nuclear plant.

Prairie Island is one of two plants in Minnesota using the water of the Mississippi to cool atomic reactors. The heat from the plant, along with other industries, makes the river warmer at Red Wing. Now ice seldom forms there.

The Prairie Island plant is owned by Northern States Power Company. The houses near the top of the picture are part of the Prairie Island Indian community.

Prairie Island

Just beside the nuclear plant is the Prairie Island community of Dakota Indians. The plant was built in 1968, but Indian people have made homes on this sandy stretch of land since ancient times. A thousand years ago gardens and cornfields surrounded a town on Prairie Island.

It was a good place to live. The land is rich and flat and the soil is soft. The bluffs shelter it from cold winds that blow across the uplands, so the climate is a little warmer and wetter in the river valley. By the year 1300 on the calendar we use, people had built other towns nearby. Some stood beside the Cannon River and some on the Wisconsin shore. At that time more people probably lived around Red Wing than anywhere else in what is now Minnesota.

When white travelers came along the Mississippi 400 years later, people who called themselves Dakota lived by the river. One of their settlements was at the foot of Barn Bluff. There a group of families shared big summer houses made of bark. Behind these were gardens planted with corn and squash. The leader of the village was known by the title of "the Red Wing."

In the 1830s Christian missionaries came to live there. Twenty years later, when white men took the land by treaty, most of the Dakota tribe moved to a reservation in western Minnesota. But the families at Barn Bluff still clung to their homes.

Archaeology *(AR-kee-OL-a-jee)* is the study of evidence from the ground. When there are no books or other written records, we depend on archaeology to tell us about the past. This and oral tradition are the main ways we learn about very ancient times.

Many bits of evidence have been found near Red Wing. The hoe above was made from a buffalo's shoulder bone. We learn much about early Indian people from such objects. We learn even more from where they were found, how deep they were buried, and what was found near them.

Even the soil tells us things. With a microscope we can find grains of seed and pollen. These show what kinds of plants grew in a place a thousand years ago. Or they may tell what was once stored in a pot long since broken.

Amos Owen of Prairie Island, shown in the early 1980s, is a pipe carrier, or holy man, of the Dakota. His ceremonial pipe is of stone.

Frances Densmore

White settlers laid plans for a town there in 1853. It was early spring, and the Dakota were away on a hunt. One day at about lunch time, a cry of "Fire!" rang out. Jumping up from their tables, the settlers saw smoke and flames pouring from the Indian houses. Joseph Hancock, one of the missionaries, said "Nobody seemed to know what to do. All stood looking as if paralyzed. In less than an hour all the bark-covered houses disappeared." Someone had set them afire, but no one would admit doing it.

When the Dakota returned and found their homes burned, some of them moved to the low islands across and up the river. The land there sometimes flooded. It was hard to reach except by boat. So white settlers looked elsewhere. Indian families could live there for a while without being disturbed.

Over the years the little settlement grew. The government forced nearly all Dakota Indians out of Minnesota in 1863, but a few were allowed to stay. Others returned quietly from time to time. By 1887 about a hundred lived in the river valley near Red Wing. Five years later the U.S. government gave them land on Prairie Island.

Today more than three hundred people belong to the Prairie Island community, but less than half of them live there. Like Minnesota's ten other Indian reservations, Prairie Island does not have enough jobs for all its people. To find work, many of them must move to cities. Still, they keep coming back. Family ties and traditional Dakota religious beliefs are strong.

Frances Densmore was an ethnologist. She spent most of her life studying the music and ways of American Indian people. Once she said: "I heard an Indian drum when I was very, very young, and I have followed it across the continent." The drum she first heard was played by one of the Dakota who lived near Red Wing.

The Densmore family moved to Red Wing in 1857. Frances was born there ten years later. As a young music teacher she became interested in Indian songs. Later she visited tribes all over the country to learn and record their music. She also made Indian friends at Prairie Island. Women like Susan Windgrow (*Ma-to-wa-śte-win* or Good Bear Woman) and Dorine Blacksmith (*Wi-kan-hpi-wa-śte-win* or Good Star Woman) taught her many Dakota songs and customs.

Susan Windgrow (left) shows Frances Densmore a Dakota mocassin. This photograph was taken in the 1930s.

When work began on the Prairie Island power plant, the Dakota hoped for new jobs. Many were hired to help build it, but now only five or six work there. Two are among the trained people who operate nuclear reactors. In 1984 Prairie Island, like many other Indian reservations, opened a bingo parlor. Crowds came from the Twin Cities. Now some people hope bingo will bring money and better times. Others are not sure. Ramona Jones, who grew up on Prairie Island, shakes her head. "Bingo won't last long," she says. "We need more different kinds of work."

A Town That Minds Its Business

The city of Red Wing reached out in 1970 to take in all of Burnside Township, including Prairie Island. There were many reasons. The new power plant was one. In 1987 it still paid nearly two-thirds of the city's taxes and gave jobs to more than 250 people. If the citizens are uneasy at having such a close nuclear neighbor, they do not talk about it much. The plant has been important to Red Wing's recent growth.

In 1970 the town had 10,400 people. In 1987 there were 4,000 more. According to Mayor Joanell Dyrstad, "There has been a tremendous resurgence here during the past ten years." But unlike Hastings, 25 miles north, the town is not yet part of the spreading Twin Cities area.

The Red Wing area. The boundary between Wisconsin and Minnesota follows the main channel of the Mississippi.

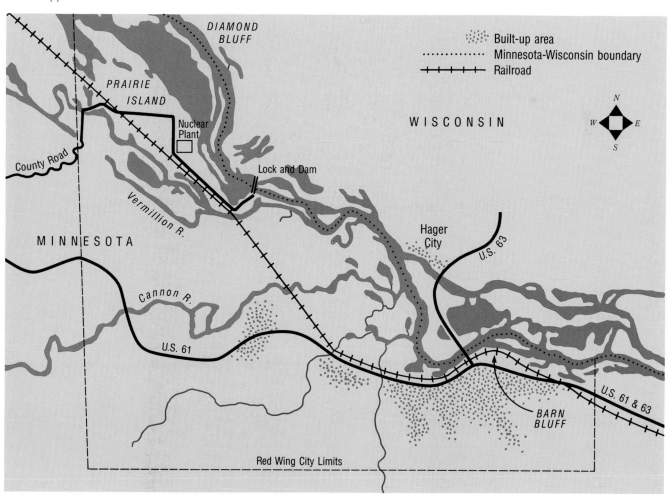

Silas B. Foot

Red Wing has always depended on its own industries. Its earliest settlers were from the northeastern states, where many people made a living in small mills and factories and workshops. In their new home they naturally did the same thing. Later immigrants came from Sweden, Germany, and Ireland. Some were skilled craftsmen. Those who found jobs often helped new people from the same country get work in the same business.

When wheat was the main crop of southeastern Minnesota, Red Wing was an important flour-milling center. But by the 1880s even the rich soil of Goodhue County was wearing out. Farmers had to grow something else or move on. Many of them went to the Red River Valley in northwestern Minnesota. Like the farmers who stayed, millers in Red Wing looked for different things to produce.

Some townspeople had already started other industries. One was Silas Foot. He was from Pennsylvania, where his father was a farmer and shoemaker. Although Silas was only 22, he had invented and sold a new kind of mechanical pump. He had money to invest and was hoping to build his own business. First he opened a store that sold boots and shoes. Then he hired people to make them. Later he started a tannery to make leather for the shoes. Today, more than a hundred years later, shoemaking is Red Wing's biggest industry, and the S. B. Foot Tanning Company is still supplying leather for it.

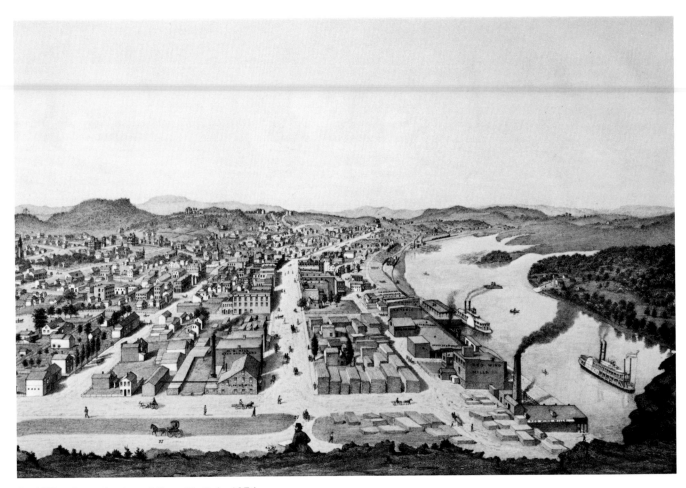
Red Wing from the top of Barn Bluff, in 1874

Over the years businessmen in the town made farm equipment and machinery. They made bricks and barrels. They quarried stone. They built boats and brewed beer. They made lumber and lime and sewer pipe. They started a furniture factory. They produced pottery, made poles for power lines, and printed diplomas. They even collected clamshells from the river for making buttons.

Red Wing also became a center for shopping and services. Its lawyers, doctors, stores, and hotels served both sides of the Mississippi. In 1895 a bridge replaced the ferry that had carried people across the river. Today nearly a third of the cars on Red Wing streets have Wisconsin licenses.

Much of Red Wing's new growth is in this kind of business. The hospital and health centers employ nearly 700 workers. Fast-food places have sprouted along U.S. 61, and there is a new shopping mall on the edge of town. In 1977 the crumbling St. James Hotel on Main Street was restored to look as it had in earlier days. Since then it has served hundreds of tourists. Some of them come just for a touch of old-fashioned style at the St. James. Others enjoy boating or fishing on the river or go skiing in winter.

The St. James is special to Red Wing. It was not rebuilt by a national motel chain. Fixing it up was the idea of William D. Sweasy, the head of Red Wing Shoe Company. People see it as one more example of the town depending on itself.

The Red Wing Stoneware Company, shown here about 1885, was one of three firms making heavy pots and jugs of local clay. Later they joined to form Red Wing Potteries.

"We Like It the Way It Is"

Restoration of the St. James Hotel made citizens take a fresh look around. Red Wing is one of Minnesota's oldest towns. During the prosperous years of wheat farming and steamboating, its people built fine, solid houses and handsome public buildings. Many of them are still there. Now Red Wing is trying to preserve them.

Concern for the environment is not new in Red Wing. Eighty years ago the operator of a stone quarry started to blast away the side of Barn Bluff with dynamite. Citizens protested that he was ruining the town's beautiful landmark. He answered that it was private property. After much argument, the destruction was stopped. To keep it from happening again, some citizens bought the bluff and gave it to the city for a park.

Red Wing people had reason to fear that the dirt and pollution from the town's many industries would in time destroy its beauty. They worked hard and spent money to keep the place clean. In recent years they have led Minnesota in finding ways to use waste products. A new city incinerator supplies steam to the leather factory. With help from the town, Northern States Power Company has converted an old electric power plant to burn trash instead of coal. Now garbage from the Twin Cities is turned into energy at Red Wing.

Alexander P. Anderson was a scientist and inventor. His parents were among many Swedish immigrants who settled in Goodhue County in the 1850s. First Anderson was a country schoolteacher. But he wanted to learn botany, the study of plants. So he saved up money and went to the University of Minnesota. Later he studied in Germany.

Anderson worked with cereal grains such as rice and wheat. In 1902, he discovered how to use heat and pressure to puff up the starch in those grains. The idea put puffed wheat and puffed rice on America's breakfast table.

In 1916 Anderson built a home and laboratory near Red Wing. He called the place "Tower View." For many years he worked there to improve the methods for making breakfast cereals. Tower View is now used by the Red Wing Area Vocational Technical Institute for environmental education.

In 1986 the citizens were asked to think about the future. How did they want their town to look in the year 2000? The answer was very clear. They wanted it to grow—but not too fast. They could do without tall buildings or big factories owned by someone far away. They did not want a freeway to Minneapolis and St. Paul. They wanted Red Wing to stay the way it was—clean and quiet, a small city between the river and the tall bluffs. They wanted it to remain a place where people felt at home and took care of the town and depended on each other.

When people stopped buying stoneware like the pieces at left, Red Wing Potteries turned to making dinnerware and vases, like those below. Many collectors prize Red Wing pottery, which is no longer made.

Chapter 2
Hawley: A Farm-Centered Town

In the Red River Valley

When you drive through western Minnesota, two sure signs tell that you are coming to a town. One is a water tower. The other is a grain elevator. Both usually rise above the trees hiding other buildings. Approaching Hawley from the east on U.S. Highway 10, you can see these two landmarks on the other side of a small valley.

The double-lane road goes down to cross a quiet-looking stream called the Buffalo River. Then it ducks under a wide railroad bridge and climbs a long, easy hill past scattered signs and business buildings. They are the kind one often sees along a highway at the edge of town. There are dealers in cars and farm equipment, a sand and gravel company, and a steak house. Soon you realize that the water tower and grain elevator are already behind. You have bypassed most of Hawley.

Looking ahead from the top of the hill, you see much farther than before. The land slopes away to the west and begins to flatten out. You are at the edge of the Red River Valley. Driving on, you pass several low ridges, with piles of sand and gravel among the trees. Beyond, the land becomes flat as a floor. It is not hard to believe it was covered with water thousands of years ago.

Today the Red River Valley is one of the world's richest farm regions. It stretches along the western edge of Minnesota and the eastern edge of North Dakota and reaches into the province of Manitoba in Canada. The river flows north to Lake Winnipeg and finally empties into Hudson Bay. Red River people live in different states and two countries, but they all belong to "the valley."

Early travelers across this land told of grass nearly tall enough to hide a man on horseback. Buffalo roamed there, and Indians hunted them. The other buffalo hunters of the valley were a people called métis (may-tee). These were descendants of Frenchmen who had come from eastern Canada to work in the fur trade. Some married Indian women and stayed in the West. Their children and grandchildren lived in settlements along the Red River.

The tracks of the Burlington Northern cross over U.S. Highway 10 as they enter Hawley. Above the trees are the grain elevator and water tower that mark most towns in western Minnesota.

Like Indian people, the métis lived by hunting animals and plants. They knew all the streams and marshes and islands of timber in the great flat sea of grass. They knew its snowstorms and floods and prairie fires and the wind that seemed to blow across it all the time. They did not try to change it or to raise crops on the land.

A Town beside the Tracks

Hawley was not there when buffalo roamed in the valley—not even its beginnings. Like nearly all the towns and farms of western Minnesota, Hawley started with the railroad. That was a little more than a hundred years ago. To help get railroads built, the government gave railroad companies great stretches of free land. After the tracks were laid across the state, trains loaded with immigrants rolled along them. The cars also carried farm machinery, lumber for buildings, and all the furniture and household goods that people brought with them.

To sell their land and to have freight and passengers for their trains, the railroad companies wanted to fill the country with farms as fast as possible. Farmers would need services, so a company would locate a depot every few miles and lay out the streets and lots of a town around it. Then the company sold the lots to businessmen.

Ten thousand years ago the Red River Valley lay beneath a huge lake—the biggest in North America. It covered not only the valley but also most of southern Manitoba. Lakes Winnipeg and Manitoba are all that remain of it now.

This ancient lake was fed by melting glaciers. After the glaciers disappeared, the lake dried up. It is called Lake Agassiz (AG-uh-see), after naturalist Louis Agassiz.

Over thousands of years many layers of mud settled to the bottom of Lake Agassiz. Today that mud is wonderfully fertile soil. Along the edges of the lake, the action of waves built up low ridges of sand and gravel. These "beach lines" can be seen at many places in the Red River Valley. One is just west of Hawley.

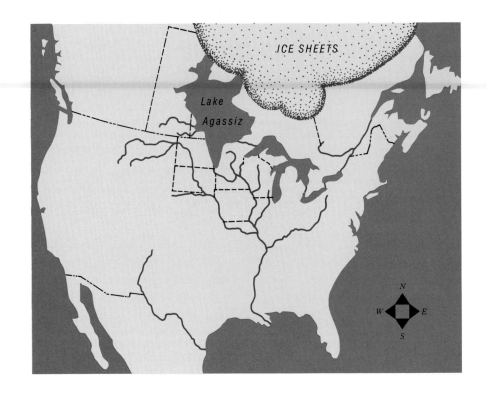

Older Minnesota towns like Red Wing looked toward rivers. The towns in the western part of the state faced railroad tracks. Often the iron rails ran straight through the middle of town, with a street on either side. Stores, lumberyards, warehouses, hotels, a bank, and other businesses lined up along the tracks. On streets leading away from the tracks were homes, churches, and schools.

Hawley was one such town, laid out by the Northern Pacific Railroad. Its original plan was just like that of Glyndon, ten miles along the tracks to the west, and Moorhead, another ten miles on. But towns, like the people in them, do not always grow according to plan. Hawley's Sixth Street, which went across the tracks and not along them, in time became the main business center. Years later the line of the railroad was changed so the tracks no longer went straight through the town.

Even Hawley's name came from the railroad. The first group of settlers arrived from England. They wanted to call their new home Yeovil (YO-ville). But on the maps and timetables of the Northern Pacific, it was Hawley. Thomas Hawley Canfield, a company officer, chose the name. So the town joined the many Minnesota places named by and for men who built the railroads. Others were Brainerd, Crookston, Moorhead, Morris, Warren, and Willmar.

A Northern Pacific engine, photographed in 1870

Looking west from the top of Hawley's grain elevator, you can see how the town was first planned. The track here used to be the main line of the railroad. Crossing it in the foreground is Sixth Street.

"The Soil Will Grow Almost Anything"

Early in 1873, when Hawley was not much more than a depot with a post office, Jesse Hayward wrote a letter. He intended it for friends in England who wanted to move to the Red River Valley. "I think the soil will grow almost anything," he said. But: "There is no getting over the fact that the winters are very severe."

Fifteen-year-old Margit Lien would have agreed. It was snowing when she and her parents and brothers got off the train at Hawley in the middle of October 1880. They were from Norway and were happy to greet friends who had come ahead of them to the Red River country. One friend offered the family a place to stay for a few days. "We were thankful," Margit remembered, "but oh, how desolate it looked as we drove. The prairie was burned and there were little log houses with sod roofs here and there." By the time they reached the friend's farm, a blizzard had begun. For two days they were snowed in.

One of the houses Margit saw may have belonged to the Burrills. They had come from New Hampshire several years earlier. Gertrude Burrill was six years old when she stepped off the train in Hawley, clutching a basket with her pet kitten. At first the family stayed in a tent. They lived through the winter in a one-room house near the depot. Gertrude's father worked as a carpenter and her mother cooked meals for the railroad crews. In the spring they moved to a farm outside of town.

The granddaughter of a Norwegian immigrant family drew this picture of the log cabin where they settled. It stood about ten miles west of Hawley.

Years later, Gertrude said: "I recall the buffalo bones and skulls on the prairie; the grass everywhere; the many sloughs, the immensity of the sky and the homesickness of my mother. She so longed for the sight of Mount Monadnock, the big white houses, and the trees, to say nothing of her mother, brothers, and friends. She died in the fall of 1874, and we took her home to be buried in the family lot. We spent the winter of 1874–75 in New Hampshire, but in the spring, we came back."

People arrived from many different places, but the greatest number by far were from Norway. Some, like the Lien family, came straight to the Red River Valley. Many others were from Norwegian settlements in southeastern Minnesota and northern Iowa. The family of Hans Tatley had moved from Trondheim, Norway, to Decorah, Iowa. The best land there was already taken. After a few years they decided to move on.

Hans, who was 17 when they made the trip, recalled: "We traveled with two yoke of oxen, a team of horses and a covered wagon. Behind our wagon we drove six cows, a few sheep, and a lone pig. These animals walked all the way from Decorah. It was a slow and tedious journey." At last, eight miles north of Hawley, "my father sighted a large grove of fine oak timber. Down a hill near the grove was a nice little lake. Here our long journey came to an end."

The flatness of the Red River Valley can be seen in the wheat fields near Hawley. Here the wheat is piled in shocks, ready for threshing. Today a single machine, called a combine, cuts and threshes wheat.

"The Lifeblood of the Village"

From its first years, the growth of Hawley has been tied to the farms around it. As Robert Brekken, editor of the *Hawley Herald,* writes: "The soil's produce has been the life-blood of the village." When farmers prosper, so does Hawley. In times of farm depression, the town is poor.

In the 1880s the Red River country became the nation's breadbasket. For years railroad cars carried great loads of wheat from the valley to flour mills in Minneapolis and other cities. But even though the fertile soil produced large crops, the farmers were not always happy. Some thought the railroads charged too much. Some felt that large milling companies agreed with each other to keep down the price they paid for wheat. Farmers held rallies and formed new political parties. They claimed that the regular Democratic and Republican parties did not represent them fairly.

Like others in the Red River Valley, farmers near Hawley planted wheat, but they also had different crops. They kept pigs, chickens, and some cows. In the early 1900s they learned that the soil around Hawley was fine for growing potatoes. Family potato patches quickly spread into large fields.

By the 1920s more than a thousand railroad cars of potatoes were loaded at Hawley each year. In the fall, town schools closed so that students could help with the harvest. Leona Anderson, who grew up on a farm a mile north of Hawley, remembers that the "potato vacation" came right at World Series time. Digging potatoes was hard work. "My back still

Where grain is harvested or shipped, it is also stored. At first it was poured into sacks and stacked in warehouses. This was slow and costly. When railroads began to transport thousands of bushels of wheat in the 1870s, they found a new way to handle it. Since then grain elevators have been part of Minnesota's landscape.

Grain elevators are storage buildings. At first they were made of wood covered on the outside with sheets of iron, to prevent fire. In later years they were often made of steel or concrete. They are called elevators because of the machinery that carries the grain from a wagon or truck to the top of the building. The earliest elevators had a chain of buckets attached to a leather belt. It was driven by a steam engine or sometimes by a horse on a treadmill. At the top the grain was dumped into tall bins. The bins were shaped at the bottom like funnels. When a bin was opened, the grain poured from a chute into a waiting railroad car.

An early grain elevator can be seen in this picture taken from the corner of Sixth and Front streets about 1909.

aches when I think of it," she says. The potato boom lasted until the 1940s. Then a plant disease, potato blight, wiped out the crop. So Hawley area farmers turned again to raising a variety of things.

But times were changing for farmers everywhere. Gasoline tractors had replaced horses. As farm machinery became bigger and more powerful, it did more work. It also cost more. Those who owned small farms could no longer keep up. More and more people sold their land and went to work in cities. Farms became larger, but there were fewer farmers.

From the 1950s to the 1970s small-town businesses related to farming also closed or moved to cities. The Hawley creamery shut down when milk from the area was trucked to Moorhead. Once cattle were butchered in Hawley. Now they are sent to meat-packers in Fargo. The town had a chicken hatchery, but people stopped raising chickens. Eggs could be bought for less from growers who had thousands of chickens in automated poultry houses. Everything seemed to be getting bigger and faster. Like most small towns in the farm belt, Hawley suffered.

The 1980s were worse for farmers than any time before. Crops were good, but prices were so low that farmers often spent more to raise grain than they could sell it for. By then only one of Hawley's three grain elevators was still in business. Farmers came in to discuss prices and crops. Sometimes they stopped along the highway at the farm implement dealer to look at new machinery. Or they drank coffee at one of the town cafes and talked about neighbors who were going broke.

Knud Wefald (Nute Wee-fawld) was one of the men sent by Red River Valley farmers to speak for them in the U.S. Congress. He had come from Norway when he was 18. After working for ten years as a farmhand, he became manager of a lumberyard in Hawley. Soon he was elected mayor of the town, and then he went to the state legislature.

During the 1920s Wefald joined Minnesota's Farmer-Labor party and ran for Congress. Twice his neighbors elected him. It was a time of depression for farmers, and he worked hard to get the government to help them. But Congress would not listen. Later, as the depression grew worse, he saw great dangers ahead. "To keep the farmer in possession of his farm is the biggest thing that must be accomplished in the United States today," Wefald declared.

Modern grain storage buildings now stand at the corner of Sixth and Front streets in the center of Hawley.

Between 1980 and 1986 the county around Hawley lost many farm families. The land is still there, but the people who lived and worked on it are gone. To some it seems that the dreams and hard work of the early settlers have come to nothing.

Hawley Looks Back —and Ahead

The town has hung on. There is nearly always a place to park in front of the empty stores along Sixth Street. Although the main line of the railroad (now called the Burlington Northern) still goes through Hawley, it has been years since passenger trains stopped there. But in the early 1970s a four-lane highway opened along U.S. 10 to Moorhead and Fargo, 20 miles away. A housing development was built on Hawley's west side, and a number of people who worked in the urban area moved there.

They found Hawley a good place to live. It has a community center with a pool. There is a park and a fine golf course that brings players from many miles around. The town has always been proud of its schools. In 1986 it added new wings to both the elementary and high schools. An annual rodeo has replaced the farmers' fairs of a hundred years ago. Hawley also holds yearly art shows that draw people from all over the region.

A young waitress at the Norseman Supper Club in 1986 talked about growing up in Hawley. She admitted she often wondered why her parents didn't leave. Teenagers, she said, go somewhere else as soon as they have

Farmers have a cup of coffee in a Hawley cafe.

a car—to the beaches of Detroit Lakes in summer, to the bright lights of Fargo in winter. But after living in one or two other places, she decided she liked the friendliness of Hawley.

A printing plant and several other industrial firms appeared in the 1970s. Another business doing well in the town is Carl's Norwegian-Maid Lefse. Lefse (LEFF-suh) is a kind of flat potato bread. The company supplies it to restaurants and supermarkets across Minnesota. It is popular wherever there are Norwegians.

In other ways, too, Hawley, along with the rest of the Red River Valley, keeps on reminding the world of its Norwegian roots. In 1971 a Moorhead schoolteacher named Bob Asp got the idea of building a Viking ship and sailing it to Norway. With the help of friends, he started cutting trees and sawing boards. At first they could find no place to build the ship. Then someone suggested Hawley, where several warehouses once used to store potatoes had been standing empty for years.

Soon one of the potato warehouses became the "Hawley Shipyard." Hundreds of people came to watch the project and help with it in different ways. The people of Hawley helped the most. In 1980 the ship was finally done. The only way to get it out was to tear the building down. So the Hawley Shipyard was gone, but the beautiful ship was wheeled to the center of town. At a great celebration, it was christened *Hjemkomst* (Yem-komst), which means homecoming.

Sign for the Norseman Supper Club

Packing lefse

Bob Asp died soon after that. His family and friends sailed the *Hjem-komst* across the Atlantic Ocean to Norway. Since then it has been seen by thousands of people. It is now on display in the Heritage-Hjemkomst In-terpretive Center at Moorhead. There it reminds visitors of the tide of Norwegian immigrants who left the rocky mountains and seashore of their native country to come to the Red River Valley.

Bob Asp and two young helpers at work on the Hjemkomst *in the summer of 1979*

The Hjemkomst *nearing the coast of Norway*

Many people like to believe that Norwegian sailors and warriors called Vikings once visited Minnesota. The story started in 1898 when a Swedish farmer near the town of Kensington was digging up a tree. Beneath its roots was a large flat stone with carving on it.

The carving turned out to be a message in the old Norse writing called runes. It told of a party of Swedes and Norwegians who had reached Minnesota in 1362. People still disagree about whether the message is a fake. Most historians think someone put it there as a joke. A neighbor of the farmer who found it claimed he had helped the farmer carve it.

Others argue that Vikings could have sailed through Hudson Bay and come by lakes and rivers to western Minnesota. They claim to have found things left there by Vikings. The most common are mooring stones—large rocks with holes drilled in them. Vikings are said to have tied their boats to such stones. One boulder thought to be a mooring stone was found a little way south of Hawley.

Chapter 3
Hibbing: A Town Built on Iron

On Top of the Hill

The city of Hibbing sits on top of Minnesota's invisible hill. Two miles from the town is the spot geologists have marked as the state's three-way divide. From there water flows to the Atlantic Ocean, the Gulf of Mexico, and Hudson Bay. The divide is on a long hump of land that stretches for almost a hundred miles through the northeastern corner of Minnesota. Ojibway Indians called this ridge of high ground Mesabi (Me-SAH-bee), which means giant. Today Minnesotans call it the Range. Beneath it once lay some of the richest iron ore on earth.

The only hills you can see around Hibbing are tall, flat-topped ridges of red dirt, piled up through many years of iron mining. At the very edge of town is one of the holes from which the red hills and the ore came. It is the largest open-pit iron mine in the world. If you did not know it had been a mine, you might think it was a natural canyon several miles long, with a lake at the bottom.

You can see more canyons like this along the Mesabi Range, both east and west of Hibbing. These great open pits were once alive with workers and machines. They dug out ore and piled it into railroad cars. Trucks hauled away gravel and dirt that covered the ore. Pumps kept water from filling up the holes. Now the power shovels and long trains of ore cars are gone. Green bushes and trees are beginning to hide the scarred rock around the edges of the pits. The pumps are still, and water birds are discovering that new lakes have formed.

Many of the people who helped dig the mines still live and work on the Range. The rich ore is gone, but there is iron in the hard rock called taconite lying beneath the Mesabi. The towns that grew with the mines are still there, too—places like Coleraine, Calumet, Nashwauk, Chisholm, Buhl, Mountain Iron, Virginia, Eveleth, and Biwabik. Some of them started as mining camps or as communities, called locations, where mining companies supplied housing and some public services for the families of workers. The towns are spread along the Mesabi Range like beads on a string. Hibbing, almost in the middle of the Range, is the largest.

Iron mining has reshaped the landscape of northeastern Minnesota. This lake on the edge of Hibbing is in what was once the Hull-Rust-Mahoning Mine. The pit, more than three miles long and up to two miles wide, was created when several mines ran together to become one big hole.

"I Believe There's Iron under Me"

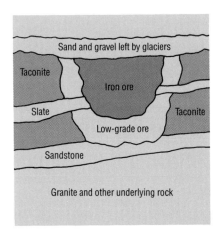

The layers of rock beneath the Mesabi Range can be pictured as a chocolate layer cake. The frosting on top is sand and gravel. Inside are thin layers of slate and sandstone. The cake itself is a rock called taconite. Buried here and there, just under the frosting, are chips of pure chocolate—deposits of rich iron ore.

Taconite is very hard rock that contains iron. The first problem is to get the iron out. This is done by crushing the taconite into powder and separating out the iron. The second problem is to put the iron in a form that steel mills can use. So it is turned into little balls, called pellets. They are the size of a large pea or a small marble.

Processing taconite takes heavy, costly machinery and many steps. These begin with blasting taconite out of the ground and carrying it to the plant. They end with loading the pellets into railroad cars and ships. Taconite plants cost a lot to build and run. They often cover acres of ground.

Early in the 1890s many prospectors were looking for iron beneath the thick pine forests that covered the Mesabi. One party headed west from Mountain Iron in January 1893. Its leader was Frank Hibbing. He had come to America from Germany at 18 and had worked on farms and in logging camps. He was an expert at telling the amount of lumber that could be made from trees. He also knew something about minerals. While looking over timber on the Mesabi for a lumber company, he had found a spot where he thought there was iron.

When Hibbing's party reached the place, they made camp in a grove of tall pines. It was bitter cold. Next morning Hibbing stepped out of his tent and called cheerily to the shivering crew: "My bones feel rusty. I believe there's iron under me." It was true. They found iron. Mining companies hurried to buy rights to the ore, and five years later Hibbing died a rich man. In the meantime he had laid out a town named after him.

Men, machines, and money poured into the Mesabi during the 1890s, and the town of Hibbing grew at breakneck speed. Mining was not the only industry. Lumbering was at its peak in northern Minnesota. Men not hired in the mines could be lumberjacks.

Lumber camps and mines needed young, strong workers for heavy, dangerous tasks. They did not have to read or even speak English. Hundreds, then thousands, of immigrants came. Most of them were single men. They were looking not for land and homes but for jobs. Many planned

This mining camp in a forest of tall pines was Hibbing in 1893.

to go back to their own countries after they had saved some money. They came from many places, but the largest numbers were from Finland, Italy, and what is now Yugoslavia.

In 1900 Hibbing was a bleak collection of unpainted buildings and pine stumps. More than 2,000 people lived there. Nearly half were men between the ages of 20 and 40, and nearly two-thirds had been born in another country. Ten years later there were almost four times as many people. It was still a rough place. The unpaved streets were lined with hotels, saloons, and boardinghouses. Standing on a corner, you might hear half a dozen languages.

In most mining towns no one cared much about improvement. Neither the company nor the workers expected to stay long. The idea was to dig iron, make money, and move on. The company owned much of the land and even many of the houses. When the ore gave out, the buildings might be moved to a new place. There seemed little reason for anyone to invest in permanent homes.

But things were beginning to change. A few of the miners had brought families with them. Some sent for sweethearts or wives they had left behind. Others married in Minnesota. People raising families wanted schools, churches, hospitals, libraries, streetlights, and playgrounds. As Hibbing grew, people who had opened stores and other small businesses also wanted improvements.

A circus paraded down Hibbing's muddy main street in 1907.

Miners were still busy in the Hull-Rust-Mahoning pit in the 1920s. Some Hibbing buildings can be seen on the far side of the canyon.

"The Richest Little Village in the World"

Hibbing led the other range towns in demanding change. In 1913 the citizens chose a young lawyer named Victor Power as mayor. He realized that mine property worth millions of dollars was inside the town limits. By taxing this property at its real value, Hibbing forced the companies to pay for making the town a better place to live. The people elected Power ten times. He made Hibbing known as "the richest little village in the world."

But a shadow hung over Hibbing's future. The great mine pits were getting closer. Everyone knew that in the end they would take the town. Hibbing stood over rich ore. People argued about it, but in the end they had to admit that America thought ore was more valuable than homes and a community.

The Oliver Iron Mining Company, which owned the biggest mines near Hibbing, took the first step by laying out a new town a mile to the south. Then it moved the houses of its workers. Most of the public buildings and businesses in old Hibbing were moved or abandoned between 1918 and 1922. What was left slowly became a ghost town. Bit by bit, from the 1920s to the 1950s, the great hole swallowed the rest of the houses.

The new Hibbing was a more solid-looking place. It had business blocks of brick and stone, a modern hotel, and fine public buildings. There were parks and boulevards. But the pride and joy of the town was its high school, built in 1921. It soon became known as the most magnificent public

Librarian Charlotte Clark, standing here beside the Hibbing bookmobile, was known as "the bus lady."

high school anywhere in the country. Its auditorium was copied from the design of a famous New York theater. The stage can hold a symphony orchestra. An audience of 1,800 can sit in the velvet-covered seats and read programs by the light of cut-glass chandeliers. The school's library is as large as that of many small colleges. The mining companies paid most of the $4,000,000 cost. Today the price would be close to $50,000,000.

To immigrant workers who had lived through hard, lonely years in the mining camps, the school stood for the future. Their dreams of going back home had faded. They knew they would spend the rest of their lives on the Range, and they would always speak English with a foreign accent. But many had children growing up as Americans. They were proud people, and improving life for the children was their main goal.

No one worked harder at that than the women. Before 1920 they could not vote. Even when they could, Hibbing and other iron range communities were slow to accept women in politics and public life. But some of them met on Saturdays in the basement of the library to discuss town issues. Women like these pioneered many improvements.

One example was a remodeled bus that took library books to people who lived at mining locations. Patricia Mestek was a child at the Kerr Location near Hibbing. She remembers the early bookmobile: "I loved it when the bus came to the corner and stopped and blew its horn until people came. It stayed about a half hour."

Victor Power made a name for himself in Hibbing by winning a court case against the Oliver Iron Mining Company. It was about a mule. Careless dynamiting in the company's mine had showered Hibbing with rocks, and the mule was hit. Its owner sued and hired Power as his lawyer.

Later, when he was mayor, Power argued: "The pine timber of our state and the iron ore were not created by the nonresident operators. They were the gift of Providence for the benefit of society." During a bitter mine strike in 1916, he stood for the rights of labor. Workers were arrested for demonstrating and picketing in some range towns, but not in Hibbing.

Not everyone liked Victor Power. Some thought him pushy and arrogant. Some accused him of dishonesty. But he is still remembered by the people of Hibbing as the "fighting mayor."

Hibbing High School, just after it was finished in 1921. Some people called it "a castle in the wilderness."

Growing Up with the Range

John and Josephine Kayfes (KAY-fus) were children of immigrants. They grew up at a mining location seven miles from Hibbing. Their parents had come from Croatia (Cro-AY-sha), now a part of Yugoslavia. Jo, the oldest, "didn't know a word of English" when she started kindergarten.

Their father was a miner, and their mother kept a boardinghouse for single men who worked in the mine. "Yes," Jo says, "we had a house full of boarders—18 of them in a 13-room house." The boarders were "all Croatian." She recalls them playing cards in the evening after the long dining table was cleared or smoking pipes and telling old-country stories.

The house, like all the others at the location, belonged to the mining company. Most of them had been moved there from another place. According to John, "I remember sleeping in one of the rooms and there was ice on the walls and we had quilts piled about five high and you had two or three or four people in a bed in order to keep warm." Carrying in wood for the stoves was the first job to be done after school.

Their mother's day began at 4:30 in the morning. It was an endless round of washing, ironing, cleaning, and cooking. "Even I had to get up," Jo remembers. "I was 12 or 13 years old. I had to get up at 4:30 to set up the dinner pails" for the men to carry to the mine. And "every Friday they would bring home their mining clothes and we'd have to wash those by hand. We were so happy when the warm weather would come, so we could go out in the yard and do our washing."

This mine crew posed for a picture during World War II. They probably wanted to show that women were doing the work of men on the "home front."

Slowly life became easier. When Jo married, her husband owned a car. John finished high school in Hibbing and went away to college. When he came back in the late 1930s he got a job in the office of the mining company. By then new federal labor laws protected miners from being fired when they joined a union. They were getting more pay, machines were bigger, and the work was safer.

During World War II men were called away to the army. The country needed steel more than ever, so the mines hired women. Most of them were the wives or daughters of miners. Ruth Dolinar (Doh-LEE-nar) was one. She remembers the overalls, the dust, and the $6.24 a day she earned. "The men didn't like it at first," she says. "We were told we could not join the union. And we were to give our jobs up when the men came back. That was agreed upon."

When the war ended the men came back to their jobs. But already a new shadow hung over Hibbing. Fighting the war had taken vast amounts of iron, and everyone knew that the ore would soon run out.

Now That the Iron Is Gone . . .

The 1950s were a grim time. Sixty years of logging and mining had made the once-green Mesabi into a barren moonscape. Towns were getting old and empty. Young people were leaving, since they saw no future ahead. One who left was the singer, composer, and poet Bob Dylan.

In 1959 Bob Zimmerman took his guitar and headed for the University of Minnesota. His life in Hibbing had been nothing unusual. He was an ordinary high school student with good grades and a special love for music. The Zimmermans owned a furniture store and attended synagogue. Like so many others in the town, they were the children of immigrants. Bob's Jewish grandparents had fled from persecution in Russia.

Early in the 1960s people across the country began to hum the tunes of a folksinger named Bob Dylan (DILL-on). The songs spoke for the civil rights movement and for protests against the Vietnam war. Bob Zimmerman had quietly changed his name and his direction in life. He had hitchhiked to New York and started to sing his own songs. Some of the most famous are "Blowin' in the Wind" and "Like a Rolling Stone."

In "North Country Blues" Dylan sang about the Iron Range:

They complained in the East,
They are paying too high.
They say that your ore ain't
    worth digging.
That it's much cheaper down
In the South American towns
Where the miners work almost
    for nothing.

The summer is gone,
The ground's turning cold,
The stores one by one they're
    a-foldin'.
My children will go
As soon as they grow.
Well, there ain't nothing here now
    to hold them.

Bob Dylan

Governor Rudolph Perpich

Then came the taconite industry. In the 1960s and early 1970s six big taconite plants joined the two that had been built earlier in northern Minnesota. Three are near Hibbing. For a while things looked bright and the Range recovered. Hibbing grew from 16,000 people in 1960 to more than 21,000 in 1980.

But soon steel mills all over the United States began to close. Steel could be made more cheaply in other countries. By 1982 there were few buyers for Minnesota taconite. Workers were laid off. It was clear that Hibbing must learn to depend on more than iron.

Some feel that tourism is the answer. The lakes and wilderness areas of northern Minnesota draw many visitors. Most of them used to bypass the Iron Range. But now nature is healing the scars on the land, and the state is helping by planting trees. The state has done more, too. It has built trails and ski areas and has opened mine tours and museums to attract tourists. Six miles east of Hibbing, Ironworld, a park and history center, tells the story of the Range. And more than 65,000 visitors come each year to see the famous Hull-Rust-Mahoning mine pit.

Hibbing welcomes them, but it is not ready to become only a tourist town. Mining and taconite still provide nearly a third of its jobs, and people look to industry for their future. Some resent the idea of being a playground for far-off cities. They look with suspicion on laws that keep mines and machines out of Minnesota wilderness areas. The best iron and

Anton Perpich left Yugoslavia in 1920. Times were hard when he came home from the army after World War I. He decided to try life in America. It was December when he got off a ship at Duluth and took a bus to Hibbing. For six years he worked in the mines and lived in a boardinghouse. Then in 1927 Anton married 16-year-old Mary Vukelich, whose parents were also from Yugoslavia. A year later Rudy, the first of four sons, was born.

Everyone in the Perpich family worked hard. When Anton was ill and could not go to the mine for more than a year, Mary scrubbed hospital floors. When Rudy was 14 he began working a night shift for the Great Northern Railway. But there was no thought of quitting school. To the Perpiches, education was one of the most important things in life.

All four Perpich sons finished college. Rudy worked as a dentist in Hibbing. Then he entered politics and became governor. He was defeated in 1978 but elected again in 1982 and 1986.

Machinery for making taconite pellets

timber are gone, but there are many willing workers left. They dream of helping America to go on growing richer and producing more.

Several companies have built small plants in Hibbing's industrial park. Town leaders point to new highways and their modern airport. They argue that Hibbing is not a far-off place in the scenic north woods. They talk with anyone who promises to bring in high-tech factories. But there have been many disappointments. "Every time we think it's hit rock bottom, we get hit again," says one longtime jobseeker.

Yet Hibbing's pride is as fierce as ever. You can see it in the community college, with its modern campus and new planetarium. You can see it in the support of school teams and sports. You can see it in loyalty to the unions that brought dignity to workers and gave them power to bargain with giant corporations. Above all, Hibbing still has pride in its immigrant heritage. Its citizens built a community from as many as 43 different nationalities. They saw that community uprooted and moved, and they built it again.

In 1976 the son of an immigrant miner from Hibbing became governor of Minnesota. Rudy Perpich was the first Iron Ranger to hold the state's top office. He speaks for the people of his own town and the rest of the Range when he says: "Wherever we are in life, we stand upon the shoulders of those who have gone before."

An air controller at the Hibbing airport

Hibbing Community College. The flat hills in the background are piles of waste dirt and gravel from mines.

Chapter 4
St. Paul's West Side:
A Stopping Place for Newcomers

Neighborhoods

More than half the people of Minnesota live in the Twin Cities metropolitan area. Flying over it, you would first notice two clusters of skyscrapers, at the centers of Minneapolis and St. Paul. All around and between them, stretching for miles, is the sea of houses, streets, railway yards, industrial buildings, freeways, shopping malls, and parking lots that make a modern metropolis. You might also see lakes, green parks, and the curving channel of the Mississippi River, in some places lined with trees.

What you would not be able to see are the neighborhoods. Even driving or walking, you might not be able to tell where one begins and another ends. No street signs would tell you. If you were to ask the people who lived there, you might get different answers. Neighborhoods are hard to define. They do not exist in laws or on maps but in minds and habits and daily lives.

You could say that city neighborhoods are communities of people who think of themselves as neighbors. Like small towns, each has a story. There may be great differences in how they look, in the way people talk, in the games the children play, and in the churches and clubs people attend.

In the twentieth century cities have become restless, shoving, fast-growing places. Everything has had to make way for more people, more industries, more cars, and new ways of doing things. Sometimes neighborhoods—especially poor ones—have been crowded out by what was called progress. That is what happened to St. Paul's lower West Side.

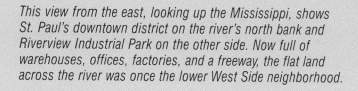

This view from the east, looking up the Mississippi, shows St. Paul's downtown district on the river's north bank and Riverview Industrial Park on the other side. Now full of warehouses, offices, factories, and a freeway, the flat land across the river was once the lower West Side neighborhood.

The Other Side of the River

What St. Paul people call the West Side is really south and a little east of the city. But it is on the west bank of the Mississippi. That was once important because for many years land west of the river was in a different territory from the country on the eastern side.

On a map of Minnesota you can see that three major rivers come together in the metropolitan area. Just below St. Paul the St. Croix joins the Mississippi from the north and east. A few miles above St. Paul, the Minnesota River comes in from the southwest. Thousands of years ago, water from melting glaciers made the Minnesota a much larger river than it is now. When it joined the Mississippi, the two streams together carved out a wide valley.

At St. Paul the valley is not as broad as at Red Wing. But across from the downtown district is a wide stretch of low, flat land. Behind this, bluffs rise in steps some way back from the river. From the tall, downtown buildings you can look south over the water and the flat land beyond. Four highway bridges and one railroad bridge connect it with the main part of the city. Cars and trucks pour across, especially over the high Lafayette Freeway. Spread out below the freeway on both sides is Riverview Industrial Park. Beyond it is the busy St. Paul Downtown Airport.

A floodwall keeps the river from rising above the low bank during times of high water. Strings of barges are moored along it. Spread out on the land behind the wall is a sample of the industries that support the Twin

The 3M Company, once called Minnesota Mining and Manufacturing, makes everything from copying machines to cellophane tape. It has a building in the industrial park.

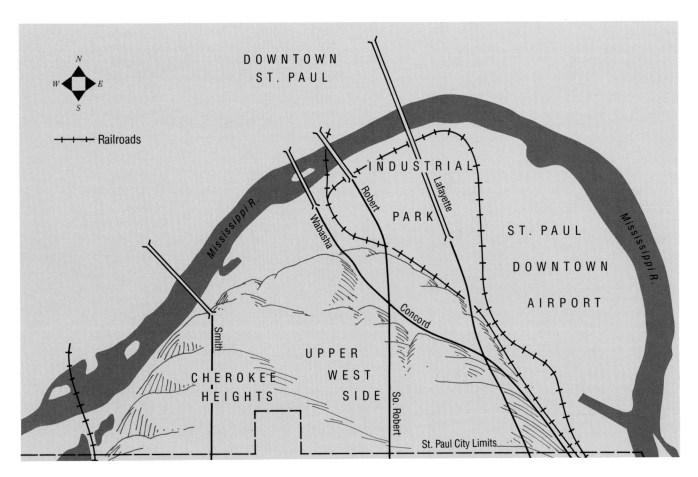

The Mississippi River makes a loop around St. Paul's West Side, cutting it off from the rest of the city.

Cities. There are warehouses and offices, banks and insurance companies, printing plants, toolmaking and electronics firms, food-processing and cold storage buildings, National Can Corporation, and Kaplan Paper Box Company. Everywhere are wide streets, parking lots, driveways, and loading docks for trucks.

Nowhere in the industrial park would you find an old shade tree or a stretch of broken sidewalk. You might never know that hundreds of people once lived on these flats and called them home. What happened? In the early 1960s the city "redeveloped" the whole neighborhood. People were moved, houses were leveled, and bulldozers erased the narrow streets.

A Vanished Neighborhood

St. Paul could give good reasons for doing this. Most of the houses were old and small. They were close together and close to the streets. Many were overcrowded and needed repair. But no one wanted to rebuild them because the flats often flooded. Services like fire protection and street repair cost the city more than it got in taxes from the area. Some called it a slum.

In the spring of 1952 the river rose higher than ever before. All the lower West Side was under water for many days. When the river went down, government engineers studied the problem. They agreed that flooding could be stopped by a floodwall or dike. But building one would be costly. No one seemed in a hurry to spend so much money to protect a run-down neighborhood.

The West Side flats in the 1890s. The Wabasha Street bridge carries traffic to downtown St. Paul.

Beneath the West Side bluffs are caves. They have been used for growing mushrooms, aging cheese, and storing beer.

While city planners and engineers talked about property values and urban renewal, people on the West Side saw other things. In spite of looking shabby, their streets were safe. Everyone knew their neighbors. Many made a living right in the community. It had no supermarkets or shopping malls or fast-food chains, but nearly every block had some small, family-owned business. There were grocery stores, butcher shops, a five-and-ten, a bakery, a pool hall, small restaurants, and corner bars.

People who had grown up there had many memories. "The West Side was just like one big family," said Frank Rangel (Rahng-HEL). "Anything that happened everybody would know right away." Ida Behr remembered: "We had many different people from many different nationalities, and a lot of freedom. Nobody ever thought of using keys." Sara Ryder agreed: "What could they steal? We were all poor."

Sara remembered sneaking with her friends into the back door of the movie theater: "The men knew us. They didn't say anything. We were kids, see. We were never in trouble. We never stole anything. So they just didn't look." She remembered other adventures, too. "One of the biggest thrills was when wagons full of over-ripe fruit went to the dump. So we would hitch on the back and go there and pick up the best fruit and take it home."

One day Sara and her friends saw a party of gypsies camped by the river. The children had heard scary stories about gypsies. They hid in the bushes because "you never knew, they might skin us or something. But we were pretty tough kids. We weren't afraid." They watched the

Yoerg's Brewery was one of the earliest industries on the West Side. This photo was taken in 1941.

48

strangers cook their food in a big pot over an open fire. Sara was glad "we didn't use their recipes," but she decided they wouldn't harm anyone.

In earlier years most families planted gardens, and many kept chickens. Some had cows. After floods, boys rigged homemade spears to catch big fish stranded in pools of water. Others hunted for crabs and crayfish along the riverbank. Some people made a living as street peddlers. There were also many salvage stores and junk dealers. Horses and wagons bringing in junk were a common sight on the West Side until the 1950s.

Newcomers and More Newcomers

Before the 1880s not many people lived on the flats. Most of those who crossed the river looked for higher ground that would not flood. Some of these early West Siders were French and Irish, but most were German. They started businesses like Yoerg's Brewery and Catholic churches like St. Matthew's. From their homes along the terraces and bluffs, they looked down over the flats onto a railroad track and a few industrial buildings.

Then one July morning in 1882 St. Paul woke up to find 200 weary, ragged refugees sitting in the railroad station. They were Jewish families who had fled from the threat of mass killings in eastern Europe. They had arrived in New York without money or friends. Someone there had put them on a train headed for Minnesota. The citizens of the city did what they could to help. To give the newcomers shelter, they set up tents on the open flats across the river. The strangers wanted to stay together, and

In about 1920 these cows belonging to neighborhood people grazed in the shadow of St. Paul's downtown skyline.

49

soon they began to replace the tents with small houses made from whatever they could find. So a Jewish community came into being on St. Paul's lower West Side.

During the next 30 years, many more refugees arrived from Russia, Lithuania, and Poland. Their language, dress, and customs seemed strange to others in St. Paul—even to many Jewish people who already lived there. In spite of being poor, they built several synagogues and a Hebrew school that were among the largest and most beautiful buildings in the neighborhood.

Meanwhile, other newcomers also found homes on the West Side. Middle Eastern people, from Syria and Lebanon, settled there in the 1890s. Some Polish people came to live along the river. There were also a few black families.

Children from all these groups studied and played together at Lafayette School. An even more important meeting place was Neighborhood House. From the early 1900s, this social settlement house offered classes in English and citizenship to new immigrants. There were also a day nursery for small children and clubs and sports for young people. Later a summer camp was started.

During World War I another group joined the neighborhood. A few Mexican men found jobs at the meat-packing plants in South St. Paul. They and their families had moved to escape the unsettled times in Mexico. In the same years Minnesota farmers began to grow sugar beets. They

Constance Currie came to the West Side in 1918. She stayed for 39 years as director of Neighborhood House. Like most early social settlement workers, she lived in the house.

People agreed that she was the best-loved person on the flats. She was acquainted with every building and family there. Many remembered her acts of kindness. They also remembered the firm way she ran Neighborhood House—and sometimes the neighborhood as well.

Standing tall and straight, she usually wore a black dress. She always insisted on good behavior. One West Sider who played at Neighborhood House as a boy says: "She was a stern lady—you didn't mess with her!" In later years, some people took to calling her "the queen of the West Side."

Constance Currie was known and respected beyond the neighborhood. In 1931 she was the U.S. delegate to a world conference on settlement work. The government of Mexico once honored her for her help to Mexican-Americans.

The day nursery at Neighborhood House during the 1930s

needed people to work in the beet fields. Many of the beet workers also came from Mexico. Whole families spent long days at the hard, low-paid labor. Manuel Contreras (Mahn-WELL Con-TRAIR-as) remembered: "It was hard in those days. There was a lot of places that didn't want Mexicans."

Most of the farm workers headed south when field jobs ended in the fall. But a few began to spend winters near the Mexican families on St. Paul's lower West Side. Often they rented houses from Jewish families who by then were moving away from the flats. Through the depression of the 1930s the little Mexican community kept growing. In the 1940s the lower West Side was mainly a Mexican neighborhood, although there were still many other people too.

Like the Jewish immigrants, the newcomers from Mexico held fast to their religious faith. The Catholic churches nearby seemed strange to them. Many could not understand the language. Early in the 1930s they formed the parish of Our Lady of Guadalupe (Gwah-da-LOO-pay), where sermons were in Spanish. Then and later it was the core of their community.

Crescensia (Cray-SEN-see-ya) Rangel recalled how the parish first rented space next to a pool hall. "Upstairs was where we started making the tacos every two weeks to raise funds for the church. Almost every month I would put on a dance and a dinner for the young people." In later times Faustino Avaloz (Faus-TEE-no AHV-a-los) and his friends belonged to the Crusaders, a church club that was "a lot like the Boy Scouts."

The sign above means "Our Lady of Guadalupe Playfield."

Lafayette School about 1915

Redevelopment and After

Through most of the 1950s St. Paul business and civic leaders talked of turning the flats into an industrial park. Still it surprised many West Siders to learn in 1960 that their neighborhood would soon be gone. They formed an association. Its president, Ruth Atkins, told a reporter from the *St. Paul Dispatch:* "The paper said we were mad. We're not mad. The old people are frightened. The young people are worried. They worry because they don't feel they get enough money for their houses. And they are sad because they are leaving a little community where everybody knows everybody else."

They had no choice. By early 1962 two-thirds of the people had moved. For some, the city built public housing on higher ground near Concord Street. Those who had money to buy or rent other homes often went higher up the hill. More than two thousand people had to leave the flats, but nearly half stayed on the West Side. This included most of the Mexican families. Still, the old community was gone.

Slowly a new West Side neighborhood formed along the bluffs. It was a mixture of people who had lived for years on the upper West Side and those who were displaced from below. In recent times they have been joined by still more newcomers, as refugee families from Southeast Asia have moved into the public housing along Concord.

Wrecking buildings in the early 1960s

Sister Mary Giovanni is a leader in the new West Side community. Her Guadalupe Area Project alternative school, started in 1965, helps students who have dropped out of other schools.

The new West Siders have overcome differences and shared memories. They have also learned to work together. In 1971 there was talk of closing the West Side's only high school and sending students across the river. The neighbors fought the closing with meetings, parades, and speeches. They won, and the new Humboldt High School was the result. Out of the campaign came a strong citizens' organization and a new community newspaper. Later they rallied to keep the West Side's branch library open and to keep a commercial ski slope from being built on the bluffs.

In recent years West Siders have tried another way of helping themselves. Shopping was a problem along Concord Street. People had to go more than a mile to buy food. They needed a good supermarket. But new stores seldom open in poor districts. So the neighbors joined to start one of their own.

Money was hard to raise, but in March 1987, after nearly three years, the 5 Corners Coop opened. West Siders saw the cooperative store as one more sign that the spirit of their neighborhood survived. And they were determined to keep that spirit alive. As an early issue of the *West Side Voice* declared: "Democracy works only if citizens take the initiative to know one another and together plan the future."

William Kuehn and his model of the old neighborhood

Juanita Gonzalez (front) and Connie Lydon were among the people working to get the 5 Corners Coop started. This picture was taken on opening day.

The West Side Citizens Organization formed a history committee in 1981. It wanted to record memories of old times on the West Side. Soon those who recalled life on the flats might be gone. People in the neighborhood would be more able to shape their future if they knew about the past they shared.

Many citizens helped. One built a scale model of the old lower West Side. Students in Humboldt High School history classes talked with old neighbors and recorded their words. They collected pictures and scrapbooks. Community leaders discussed preserving historic buildings.

Then a two-day conference was held at the school. The citizens who came learned a lot about the place they lived in and about the good and bad times that made it a community. They nodded in agreement when one speaker quoted the Czech writer Milan Kundera (MILL-ahn KOUN-deh-rah). He said: "The struggle against power is the struggle of memory against forgetting."

Unit II
Changing Worlds

Chapter 5
How Long Is a Thousand Years?

Time and Time Again

There are many ways to think about time. For early people all over the world, time often seemed like a series of circles. There was the circle of a day, beginning with sunrise. Events might be different from one day to the next, but days always went through the same kind of circle. There was also the circle of a year. Spring came, followed by summer, fall, and winter, and the circle started again with spring.

There was the circle of a human lifetime. A person was born, grew up, married, had a child, grew old, and died. The new baby went through the same circle of life. The time between birth and growing up to become a parent is called a generation. Before people had calendars or written records, this was one of the most important units of time. The time of a long-ago event was remembered by the number of generations that had passed.

People saw still other circles. The tides, the moon, the stars, the animals, and the plants moved in circles over time. It was only natural to think that history, too, moved in circles. For example, a tribe or nation might grow great and powerful, then be overcome, and another tribe would follow it through the same kind of circle. Without written records, it was hard to see whether there were permanent changes that made life different from what it had been before.

After people learned to write, their idea of time began to shift. By reading the records, they could see that some things had changed. New ideas and inventions had appeared. Life was not exactly the same through circle after circle. Slowly they began to think of time as a line made up of circles. That was the beginning of history as we know it.

As the glaciers that covered Minnesota during the last ice age melted away, huge animals roamed the country. In this scene imagined by an artist who is also an archaeologist, a band of human hunters spies a herd of mammoths. Bones of the elephant-like beasts have been found in Minnesota. No one knows for sure whether people hunted them here.

55

Signs in the Earth

These Paleo-Indian spearpoints found in western Minnesota are probably between 8,000 and 10,000 years old.

The driftless area is a small part of Minnesota that was never covered by glaciers. Currents in the moving streams of ice caused them to flow around this land. Along with nearby parts of Wisconsin and Iowa, it makes up what looks like an island on the map.

This area is called driftless because it is not covered by the layers of earth and gravel left by glaciers. Here the hills are steep and rugged, and the valleys cut deep between them. The bulldozer action of the ice never smoothed the landscape.

For a long while people thought that only human events changed. They could see no differences through time in the natural world. There the same circles seemed to repeat endlessly. But about three hundred years ago people began to study the earth and see signs that it, too, had changed. Then they started to believe that the natural world also had a history. The line of time seemed to become much longer, stretching back millions of years.

Some of the signs they found were bones of animals unlike any that live on the earth now. Some were patterns of leaves, pressed into rocks. Others were the channels of rivers where no water flowed, or flat valleys that appeared to be the beds of ancient lakes. By studying these things, scientists began to piece together the story of the earth's past.

One thing they learned was that great sheets of ice have spread down from the Arctic many times in the last million years. When the climate grows warmer, as it is now, they melt away and may be gone for thousands of years. When it gets colder again, the glaciers return. Sometimes they are many hundreds of feet thick. Their great weight presses down upon the earth. Slowly they grind rocks into sand. In some places they scrape away the soil. In others they pile it into hills.

Minnesota has been covered by these ice sheets time after time. That is why the northeastern part of the state is a rugged land of cliffs and scarred stone. Its hundreds of lakes are held in rocky cups where the moving ice scraped away the earth. That is why most of southern Minnesota is

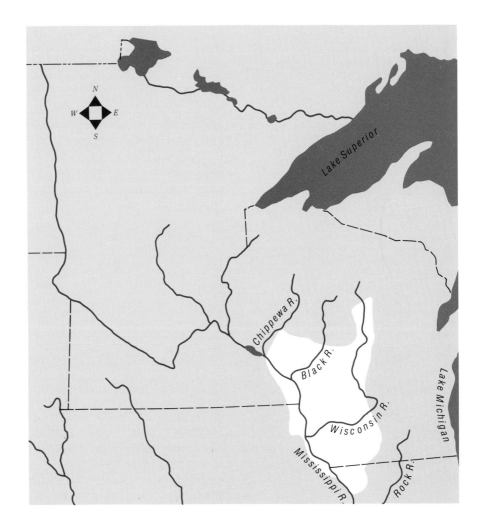

covered with soil many feet deep. It was left there by the glaciers when they began to melt.

The ice last moved southward about a hundred thousand years ago. By 10,000 years ago it was melting, but northern Minnesota was still partly covered. As the ice turned to water, it made foaming rivers and lakes like great puddles hundreds of miles wide. On the shores of the lakes and along the edges of the ice grew dark forests, mostly of spruce. Moss covered the ground beneath. Few flowers blossomed there and not many birds sang. But in the open places grass grew and herds of large animals roamed. There were mammoths, like elephants with shaggy hair and long, curving tusks. And there were giant bison, twice the size of buffalo in later times.

The First "Minnesotans"

One day the first band of human hunters came, probably following a herd of animals from the south or southwest. We know very little about these earliest Minnesotans. Archaeologists call them the Paleo-Indians or big-game hunters. The only traces they left in Minnesota are a few stone spearpoints, skillfully chipped from hard, glassy rock.

As hundreds of years passed, the ice sheets melted away, and the lakes and rivers began to shrink. The mammoths and some of the other great animals disappeared, not only here but everywhere in the world. Maybe the hunters killed too many, or maybe the changing climate made it hard for them to live.

Early hunters begin to skin a mammoth. The people at right are mending weapons and making spearpoints.

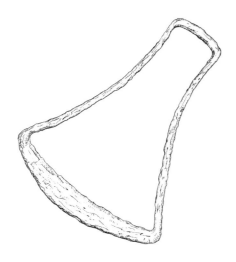

This ancient copper knife, found in Cass County, is a little longer than a pencil. It was made in what archaeologists call Archaic times, from 2,500 to 8,000 years ago.

By 7,000 years ago the climate had grown warmer than it is now. Most of the dark, pointed spruce trees had died. Birches and pines grew in their place. Then came maple, oak, and other trees, along with many kinds of bushes and flowering plants. More flowers and seeds brought more insects, birds, and small animals. As the lakes and streams became warmer, water plants grew, making food and homes for more kinds of fish, along with turtles and frogs.

The way people lived changed, too. Life was easier. They still hunted large animals, but they also picked nuts and berries and caught small animals like rabbits and squirrels. Sometimes they speared fish in shallow streams or through holes in the ice during winter. As several thousand years went by, newcomers may have moved in from farther south. Some of them probably brought along new ideas.

Slowly the ways of making tools and weapons changed. People began to shape stone by grinding and polishing it as well as by chipping. In this way they could make heavy axheads, strong enough to cut wood. Another important idea was the use of metal. In the country around Lake Superior were natural chunks of almost pure copper. People learned to search for the soft, tough nuggets and to pound and shape them into spearpoints, knives, and awls. They were the first Americans to make things of metal. That was around 5,000 years ago.

The base of the spear fits into a notch in the end of the modern model of an atlatl above. When the thrower swings the stick forward with a snapping motion, the spear flies with great force. The feathers on the spear, like those on an arrow, help it go straight. The loop of leather around the thumb helps the thrower hold onto the atlatl. Some early atlatls had a stone weight, which increased their power. The rock carvings at left are thought to picture men with such atlatls.

Trading Ideas

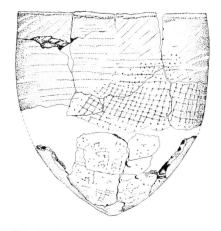

This broken clay pot was found near Gull Lake in north central Minnesota. It may be as much as 2,000 years old. The people who made it are called Early Woodland by archaeologists.

Others wanted the copper objects and offered to trade things for them—bone and ivory, skins and bright-colored feathers, or maybe a seashell from some faraway ocean beach. Trade brought more meetings of people and more sharing of ideas. Changes began to come faster.

One new idea was the atlatl (AT-lat-l). This was a hinged stick that made it possible to throw a spear faster and farther than ever before. People also began to make more things out of wood, bone, and shell. They now used the shiny copper mainly for ornaments. At some point they learned how to weave mats and baskets from rushes and cattails. Even more important was making jars and pots of clay. Minnesotans began to do this more than 2,500 years ago. After each change, others came more quickly, although to us the pace of change seems very slow.

By 1,500 years ago, people around the lakes and swamps of what is now central and northern Minnesota began to harvest wild rice and store it for winter use. With this new and dependable source of food, the population increased. At the same time, the knowledge of how to plant gardens and grow crops moved slowly north from Central America. There Indian people had begun to raise corn, beans, and squash. They also kept track of time with a calendar and built towns and cities.

Late Woodland people lived in Minnesota about 500 to 1,500 years ago. No one knows just what their dwellings looked like, but they were probably made of bark, like those shown.

A thousand years ago, people in the river valleys of southern Minnesota lived in towns surrounded by fields. For hunting animals they used bows and arrows as well as spears. To fish, they often used hooks and lines. They cooked and stored food in jars of decorated pottery. They made fine pipes of stone and wood and smoked tobacco grown in their gardens. Sometimes they traveled hundreds of miles on the rivers to trade with people farther south.

A World of Kinship

We know something about how ancient Minnesotans lived because of the things they left, long buried under layers of soil. Archaeologists have studied these objects and given names to the different life ways following through thousands of years. But we know very little about the beliefs and customs of these people or how they thought about the world. They did not write. Their dreams and memories were kept mostly in stories and songs. Some of these are still known among Indian people.

There are also other clues to what they believed about life and the world. One is the thousands of earth mounds they left. They built these to bury the dead and probably as places of worship. Some were high and cone-shaped. Some were long and low. Others were made in the forms of animals, birds, turtles, or snakes. It must have taken great labor to build them by carrying earth in baskets or bags.

This beautiful pottery jar was found near Red Wing. The designs and shape tell us it was made by some of the people who lived there 1,000 years ago. We call them Mississippian because their way of life was much like that of people farther down the Mississippi.

At one time there were nearly ten thousand such mounds in Minnesota. Most have disappeared. They have been plowed under by farmers or destroyed to make way for buildings and highways. From those that are left, we can guess that the ancient people thought a lot about the mysteries of life and death. They did not bother to build forts or roads or big houses. But they spent years piling up earth to mark sacred places and to make sure the graves of their ancestors were remembered through the many circles of time.

They also left pictures and signs. Some they painted on cliffs and in caves. Others were carved into rock. In Cottonwood County there is a low hill with a top of smooth stone. Hundreds of shapes have been scratched into it. Some seem to picture animals and people. Others are strange designs. No one knows just what they mean or why they were put there with so much patient work. But it is easy to guess that this was a sacred place.

The pictures hint of a world full of spirits and symbols and the power of dreams. So do the stories that are remembered. To these people a man was not a great hunter just because he was strong and smart and had keen eyes and a sharp spear. He also had to know the spirits of the animals and have their good will. The ancient people believed in a world where humans had a place along with every other kind of being. They were not masters of the living things or of the lakes and streams. All were part of a family. Only if people knew the rules of the world and acted like kinfolk would things go well for them and for all other beings.

Among the few burial mounds still left in Minnesota are these in St. Paul's Indian Mounds Park. They stand high on a hill above the Mississippi River.

How long is a thousand years? No one really knows. None of us has ever lived that long.

Picture a little girl with bright eyes and dark hair. Think of her growing into a young woman and having a child of her own. That child grows up and also has children. The first little girl is now a grandmother. Her grandchildren grow into tall men and women and they, too, have children. Now the little girl has become a great-grandmother. She is an old woman, bent and white-haired.

More time goes by. One day a young woman says to the little girl standing by her knee, "I remember my great-grandmother. She was very old when I knew her. When she was a little girl like you . . ."

Repeat this story ten times, and that is a thousand years.

Chapter 6
Strangers from Another World

The Sacred Circle of Life

Almost five hundred years ago reports began to spread through the countries of Europe about a new world found across the ocean in the west. By then European people believed firmly that time moved in a line. They had objects and written records from the ancient countries around the Mediterranean Sea. They knew how events there followed each other and how life changed.

For the people of Minnesota and the rest of North America, time was still made up of circles. These were formed by the ways of nature. They all moved in harmony to make an orderly world. Daily life followed this pattern of sacred circles. One was the year with its changing seasons. Each season brought a time for doing certain things.

The Dakota who lived around the headwaters of the Mississippi River moved from place to place as the seasons changed. Their country was a borderland between deep evergreen forests and open plains. It also had grassland, or prairie, dotted with groves of oak, and thick woods of maple, elm, birch, walnut, and other leafy trees. Then, as now, the summers were hot and the winters were bitterly cold.

When winter came the Dakota set up tipis (tee-pees) in the shelter of woods. They pegged the skin walls snugly to the ground and piled snow around the edges to keep out the cold wind. Women, children, and older people moved among the trees, collecting fallen branches for firewood. Men, wearing snowshoes and carrying bows or spears, went out to hunt for deer, elk, moose, and sometimes buffalo.

Usually there was game to hunt and enough fresh meat. When an animal was killed, every part of it was used—skin, fur, antlers, hooves, bones, and meat. Anything left was carefully buried, and people thanked the animal spirits for giving up their lives. The Dakota thought that if they did not do this the animals would hide. Then there might be hunger.

With warmer winds and melting snow, the Dakota rolled up the skins of their tipis and moved to another place. Many went to maple groves to draw sap from the trees and make it into sugar. Others went to streams to fish. Some hunted muskrat and beaver, whose furs were especially thick and soft at the end of winter. When flocks of ducks and geese landed on lakes and ponds on their way north, those were hunted too.

This painting done in the 1840s shows Dakota life, which probably did not look much different from two centuries earlier. Large summer houses like this one were often shared by two or three families.

Later in the spring, the people came together again, at the place where their gardens would be planted. It was usually by a river or lake, where the soil was soft and sandy. There they often had big summer houses made of poles and bark. They used these houses year after year.

The first white blossoms of wild strawberries signalled the time to plant corn. When that was done, the people turned to summer tasks. The men hunted buffalo roaming in small herds through the prairies of southern and western Minnesota. The women and children picked berries and dug roots like the wild turnip. These were eaten fresh or dried for winter use. It was also a time to gather herbs and plants for medicine. The Dakota, like other Indian peoples, knew many such remedies for illness.

As the corn grew tall, the children scared away flocks of blackbirds trying to eat the kernels. Ripe ears, roasted in the husk, were a treat for everyone. Corn was also dried and saved for winter. Sometimes the Dakota traded with other tribes for more dried corn.

Summer was the time for such trade and for sacred ceremonies, contests, and dances. Life was easy in summer. There was plenty of chance for laughter and play and making love and seeing old friends. But sometimes it also brought war among tribes over hunting rights or old grudges.

As summer turned to fall, the wild rice ripened. Most of the Dakota moved to the shallow lakes and swamps where it grew. In canoes, they pushed slowly through the beds of rice. Bending the tall stalks, they shook or beat them over each canoe until the bottom was full of rice.

The Dakota used skin tipis in the winter or when they traveled. The tipi and all household goods belonged to the women of the family.

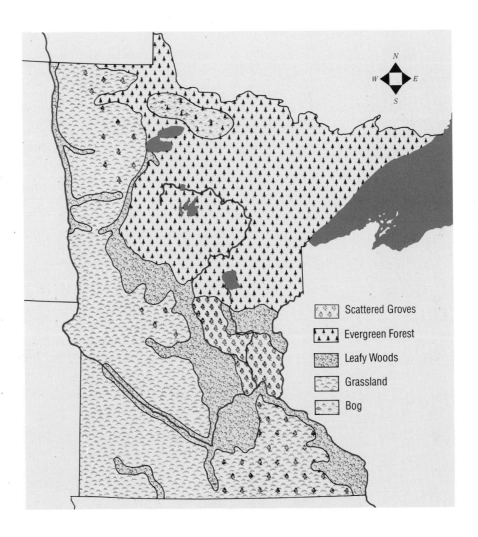

Scattered Groves

Evergreen Forest

Leafy Woods

Grassland

Bog

This map shows the kinds of trees and plants that covered Minnesota when it was the country of the Dakota.

With the first snow came the fall hunt. Then the whole band made ready to travel with the hunters. It was a time of hard work and excitement for everyone. Women, children, and older people were responsible for moving the camp each day or two. The men followed herds of deer or buffalo, trying to store up food for the cold months ahead. If they were successful, meat hung drying on outdoor racks over smoky fires. Skins piled up waiting for women to scrape and soften them for clothing.

Then the snow deepened. Feet and fingers began to grow numb with cold. Plants and small animals seemed asleep under the white blanket. So the Dakota went back again to their favorite winter places. There they gathered around the fire in the center of the tipi. The time had come for quiet tasks like making clothes and mending snowshoes.

Stories of the Elders

While they worked, the older people often told stories. It was their way of teaching the children, but everyone listened and learned. Some stories were about dreams and about the spirit world. Others were about the animals, birds, and fish that gave them food and clothing. The Dakota called living things and all the natural world *Mi-ta-ku-ya-pi,* or my relatives.

Some stories were about the people themselves. The name Dakota means friend. Seven groups of Dakota lived in the grasslands and forests around the headwaters of the Mississippi River. They called themselves *O-će-ti-śa-ko-win,* or the seven council fires.

Among the favorite contests when groups of Dakota met during the summer were ball games like lacrosse. Here the men watch while the women play against each other.

One of their favorite places in both winter and summer was near the southern end of Lake Mille Lacs. Some of them lived at Leech Lake, and others had homes in the Minnesota Valley. They believed they had always lived in the country they called *Mi-ni-ma-ko-će*. One story told of how humans first came into the world from a cave near where the Minnesota River joins the Mississippi.

One day a new story was heard. It was about strangers from the east who brought ways and wonderful objects never before known to the Dakota. At first one of the elders foresaw this in a dream. Soon Ottawa and Huron Indians from across the Great Lakes brought some of the new things. They offered to trade with the Dakota and other tribes of the West.

At last a few of the strangers themselves came along with a band of the Huron. The Dakota sent messengers with gifts to welcome them and invite them to a council. Stories about the meeting were repeated for many winters. They told of how the strangers looked—of their light skin, pale eyes, and hairy faces. They also told of a black powder the strangers threw into the fire. It made a terrible noise and sent burning sticks in all directions. Later the Dakota saw how the powder was used in guns.

The white strangers seemed friendly. But the Huron and Ottawa formed a big settlement on the south shore of Lake Superior. Without asking, they hunted animals far into Dakota country. Before many years passed, the Dakota attacked the other tribes and drove them away. The white men went, too.

This picture of women gathering wild rice was painted in the 1800s. Their way of working had not changed, but their way of dressing had. Dakota people probably learned from the Ojibway how to make birch-bark canoes like this one.

New Neighbors

Still other tribes moved westward as the Huron and Ottawa had done. The Ojibway, now often called Chippewa, pushed steadily toward Dakota country from their homes at the east end of Lake Superior. They called themselves *A-nish-i-na-be,* or The People, and they spoke of the Dakota as enemies. White men had trouble with the Ojibway word for the Dakota. It ended with a sound like *soo,* which in French was written *Sioux.* So that was what they began to call the Dakota.

The white men wanted to trade, and they urged the two tribes to make peace. In 1679 a daring French trader named Daniel Du Luth made his way to one of the main Dakota towns at Lake Mille Lacs. He and the seven white men with him were the first of the pale strangers seen by many of the Dakota.

The leaders of the tribe listened to what Du Luth said. They examined the metal tools, soft wool blankets, and other things he brought. They may also have talked about their need for guns. Other tribes, they knew, were getting the new weapons. They had reason to fear they might not be able to defend themselves. At last they agreed to a bargain. The Ojibway, they said, could live nearby and hunt in Dakota country. In return, the Ojibway would let Frenchmen travel across Lake Superior to trade with the Dakota.

No one can be certain about the first Europeans to reach the country that is now Minnesota. It seems likely they were a pair of Frenchmen named Pierre Radisson (Pe-air Rah-dee-soan) and Médard Chouart des Groseilliers (May-dar Shoe-ar day Gro-say-yay).

The two adventurers made several trips west with the Huron and Ottawa in the 1650s. On one they visited the Dakota, whom they called the Buffalo People. Historians cannot tell from their description of the country just where this was. It may have been near Mille Lacs.

Radisson wrote about their travels. He hoped to convince businessmen in Europe to open trade with the tribes of the West. His own people, the French, were not interested. But some Englishmen were. After talking with Radisson, they decided the best way to reach the western tribes was from the north. So they sent trading ships into Hudson Bay. This was the beginning of the Hudson's Bay Company, a famous fur-trading firm.

This painting of Radisson and Groseilliers and the one of Du Luth on the next page were imagined by modern artists.

Copper kettles like this one, brought by white traders, replaced bark containers like the one opposite.

Only a few months after Du Luth left, a group of Dakota men traveling down the Mississippi River met a canoe with three Frenchmen coming north. The Dakota were puzzled and suspicious. No one had said anything about white men coming from the south. So the Dakota told the three men they must return with them to Mille Lacs. One of the Frenchmen was a priest named Louis Hennepin. He and the others had to stay with the Dakota through most of the summer. Then the trader Du Luth heard about the three captives. He persuaded the Dakota to let the Frenchmen return home with him.

As years passed, other traders came. One was Pierre Le Sueur (Le Soo-er). He built a small trading station on an island near the mouth of the river the Frenchmen called St. Croix. Later Le Sueur went up the Minnesota River to a place where the Dakota said he could find bluish-colored earth. He thought it was copper ore and took some of it away with him. In France he learned it was not copper at all. The river where he found it is still called the Blue Earth.

During these years the Dakota remained at peace with their Ojibway neighbors. The two tribes spoke different languages, but their customs and ways of living were much the same. Sometimes Dakota men married Ojibway women. Sometimes Dakota women found husbands among men of the Ojibway tribe.

Daniel Greysolon, Sieur du Luth, was a French officer who had served in the king's bodyguard. He had fought bravely in a battle against the Dutch. Still, he was not rich, and hoping to make a fortune, he went to the colony of New France in what is now eastern Canada.

Soon he learned that the governor of New France wanted to open trade with the Dakota and other western tribes. Du Luth agreed to try. With seven Frenchmen and three Indians, he left Montreal in the fall of 1678. They spent the winter with friendly Ojibway at Sault Ste. Marie (Soo Saint Marie). In the spring they set out by canoe for the Dakota country. From the western tip of Lake Superior, they headed inland toward Mille Lacs.

After meeting with the Dakota, Du Luth sent messengers inviting the Ojibway and other tribes to a council. It was held near the place where the city of Duluth is now. There, in September 1679, all agreed to keep peace with each other and to let Frenchmen trade in the area.

DANIEL GREYSOLON SIEUR DULHUT
AT THE HEAD OF THE LAKES — 1679

One example of this intermarriage is the family of two famous leaders. They were White Fisher *(Waub-o-jeeg),* an Ojibway, and Wabasha *(Wa-pa-ha-śa* or Red Banner), the first of three Dakota chiefs of that name. Wabasha married an Ojibway woman. But when war started between the tribes, she and their children had to return to her people. Later she married an Ojibway man and had a son who became the father of White Fisher.

The story is told of how Wabasha refused to make war upon the band of Ojibway to which his former wife and her children belonged. Once when they met in peace, the young White Fisher, then a small child, kicked at Wabasha, thinking him an enemy. The chief admired the boy's spirit and predicted that he would grow to be a great fighter. He was right. Years later White Fisher led the Ojibway to victory in an important battle against the Dakota.

New Ways and New Wars

By the mid-1700s the Dakota began to feel even more changes. Spanish people from Mexico had brought horses into what is now the southwestern United States. Until then Indian people had not known these animals. Tribes living on the plains quickly learned how to train and ride them. Horses gave them new freedom and power. On horseback they could follow the great herds of buffalo across the grasslands. People, baggage, and supplies could be moved faster, and hunting was easier. So was warfare.

Dakota hunters spearing muskrats

Some of the Dakota bands turned eagerly to the new life on the plains. Moving westward, they gave up planting corn and harvesting wild rice to become horsemen and buffalo hunters. They also raided the towns and fields of more peaceful farming tribes in the Missouri River valley.

The Dakota who stayed in Minnesota found themselves at war, too. No longer did they need the good will of the Ojibway to get tools, weapons, and other goods from white men. French traders who followed Hennepin's route up the Mississippi sold the Dakota all they wanted. But to buy, they had to have furs, especially beaver skins from the northern streams and forests. The Ojibway had hunted there in peace for many years. They felt the country belonged to them.

In 1736 the two tribes began fighting. The off-and-on warfare lasted for more than a hundred years. Slowly the Ojibway pushed the Dakota to the west and south. By 1800 the Ojibway held all the lakes and woods of northern Minnesota—even the wild rice beds and fishing places around Mille Lacs. The eastern Dakota moved down the Mississippi below the Falls of St. Anthony and west into the valley of the Minnesota.

The place where these two rivers joined was a sacred meeting ground for the Dakota bands. There they held dances, ceremonies, councils, and contests. They called it *Mdo-te*, or the place where rivers meet. White traders who often camped there began to call it Mendota. Soon it became a center for exchanging goods and furs.

This picture painted in the 1840s shows Dakota men killing buffalo. In earlier years such hunters would not have had guns or used saddles.

This portrait of Louis Hennepin was painted after he returned to Europe.

Louis Hennepin was one of many Catholic priests who became missionaries in the French parts of North America. Hoping to teach the Indians Christianity, he joined an expedition led by Robert Cavelier, Sieur de la Salle (Ro-bair Ca-vuhl-yay Seoor day la Sal). They traveled west through the Great Lakes. From a winter camp in Illinois, La Salle sent people ahead to explore the country. He chose Hennepin and two others to travel up the Mississippi River. There they met the Dakota.

The Dakota treated Hennepin well, but it was early spring and they did not have much food. He often went hungry. Later he wrote: "Although the women showed more tenderness and pity than the men, their scant supply of fish was given to their children." He did not blame them.

Trying to learn their language, Hennepin wrote down the Dakota words. The Indians felt this gave him some special power. But not many would listen to his talk about the Christian God. After he had gone back to France, the priest wrote a book about his adventures. It made him famous and taught many people in Europe about the upper Mississippi Valley.

While Hennepin was traveling with the Dakota, they passed a waterfall on the Mississippi. It probably looked much like this painting. He called it the Falls of St. Anthony in honor of his favorite saint.

Chapter 7
The Fur Trade: Where Two Worlds Meet

Trading More Than Goods

The first and most important way in which Europeans and Native Americans learned about each other was through trade. Each group wanted things the other had. And each thought it was getting a bargain. Neither one had any idea of changing the way it lived. Indians wanted things that would make it easier to do what they had always done. European traders wanted to make money. In the end both sides found themselves different. They exchanged much more than material goods.

From the late 1600s until the early 1800s long lines of canoes traveled each year across the Great Lakes. They carried tools, cloth, and weapons made in England, France, and other European countries. Slowly these goods changed the ways Indian people looked and worked. No longer were their clothes all made of animal skins, bark fiber, or grass. Woven cloth was more comfortable and easier to keep clean. The women had blouses and long skirts. The men wrapped themselves in blankets or coats of heavy wool. They still wore leather moccasins and carried leather bags. These were often decorated with colored glass beads from Europe.

Tribal people like the Dakota and Ojibway stopped making clay pots to cook or store food in. The brass and tin kettles brought by traders were fireproof, easy to carry, and did not break. Knives, needles, axes, and hoes of iron or steel replaced tools of stone or animal bone. Thread was easier to sew with than strips of leather. Guns replaced bows and arrows— sometimes. Guns were heavy and expensive. They needed bullets and gunpowder and often had to be repaired.

At first Indian traders like the Ottawa and Huron made and paddled the canoes that carried these goods. Soon Frenchmen and later Englishmen found they could profit more by traveling into the country themselves. They began to learn the ways of the new land. They used birch-bark canoes. They made snowshoes and toboggans for winter travel. They ate corn and wild rice and maple sugar.

Europeans also learned the routes Indian traders followed. But the journeys were long. It took all summer to travel from the East Coast to the upper Great Lakes and back. So traders had to spend winter in the West. Some stayed with friendly Indian people. Most of them built cabins for themselves and their goods and put up tall fences, or stockades.

This painting by a modern Minnesota artist shows four fur trade canoes passing through one of many connecting lakes on the Minnesota-Ontario border. This much-used canoe route became known as "the voyageurs' highway."

A Wintering Post on the Snake River

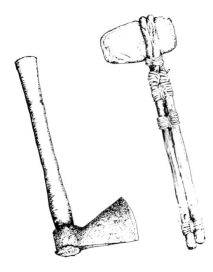

A stone ax made by Indian people, and an iron ax brought by traders

In the fall of 1804 John Sayer, probably with five canoes and a crew of about 15 men, headed for the place where he would spend the winter. By that time most traders around the Great Lakes belonged to one of several large companies. Each company had stations on the western Great Lakes. This meant the traders did not have to go all the way east to get goods and deliver furs.

Sayer was a partner in the North West Company. He had been a trader for a long time in the northern Minnesota country. His wife was Ojibway. Her name, written as *Obemau-unoqua,* probably meant woman who is a chief or leader. She traveled with Sayer on most of his trading trips.

Sayer planned to trade that winter with some Ojibway bands who lived in the St. Croix Valley. He had been there before and had promised to come back. This year he would build a post on the Snake River, a branch of the St. Croix. He started from Fort William, North West Company headquarters on the north shore of Lake Superior. His route led from Lake Superior up the Brule River and across a portage, or carrying place, to the St. Croix. He had sent two canoes ahead. Early in September he followed with three others.

Going up the Brule was hard work. Often the canoes and their cargo had to be pulled through shallow water or carried around rapids. The men did this while Sayer watched and directed them. He was the boss, or *bourgeois* (boor-zhwah). They were *voyageurs* (voy-ah-zhoors).

This map shows North West Company trading places in northern Minnesota and Wisconsin around 1804-05. It was unlawful for British traders like John Sayer to do business in U.S. territory, but there was no one to stop them.

Going down the St. Croix was less work but more dangerous. At the end of the first day, Sayer wrote in his diary: "Camp'd at 4 P.M. below the big rapid to repair 2 of the canoes. They got broke." The men patched them with birch bark. Sayer's wife and some other Indian women gathered gum (the sticky sap of spruce trees) for waterproofing the patches.

The Snake River was like the Brule. The travelers spent five hard days climbing over and around rapids. At Cross Lake they stopped to rest and repair canoes again. It was October 1, and Sayer noted that "it froze considerably last night." But they were near the end of the trip. A band of Ojibway met them there to talk with the trader and "to fix on a place for my winter's abode."

There was a day or two of celebration and drinking. Sayer, like most traders, carried plenty of liquor. Sometimes he sold it. More often he gave it to the Indians as a sign of friendship or to seal a bargain. He also rewarded his men with liquor when they had worked hard or on special holidays. But so much was used, it became a serious problem for voyageurs, Indians—and Sayer himself.

After the celebration, Sayer got back to business. Many of the Ojibway were ready to leave for fall hunting. They needed supplies. Sayer gave them goods on credit. He also bought some bags of wild rice and hired an Ojibway hunter to furnish meat for his men. Then he looked for a good spot to build a winter post.

Voyageurs were the ordinary workmen of the fur trade. They paddled canoes and hauled heavy loads on their backs for low pay. Seldom did a voyageur become a trader. English and French ideas at that time held that a trader must be a gentleman. He should be educated and come from a well-to-do family. Most voyageurs were the sons of French farmers and workers in eastern Canada. Few could read or write.

In spite of their hard, dangerous life, voyageurs had plenty of spirit. They wore brightly colored caps and sashes. They boasted of their strength. Sometimes they held contests to see who could carry the heaviest load. The skilled canoemen were greatly respected. The lives of all depended on them. To keep time in their paddling and raise their spirits, voyageurs often sang at their work. The songs were mostly old French tunes reminding them of homes and families far away.

The site he chose was on a sandy ridge along the river. His men cleared the trees, using the logs to start building. On October 15 Sayer noted with relief: "Men finished the store and put all the provisions and goods under lock and key. A good thing in time of danger."

The danger he feared was Dakota hunters. The Snake River was near the edge of Dakota country. They were unfriendly to Sayer because he traded with their enemies, the Ojibway. Sayer urged his men on, and they finished the rest of the buildings before the first heavy snowfall.

A Trader's Life

Beaver

The year turned out to be a good one for Sayer. Hunger was often a problem for traders. They could not carry much food with them, so they had to depend on getting it from the Indians. That winter there was enough. The Ojibway women had harvested a large crop of wild rice. Sayer's hunter and other Indians brought in game almost every day. In the fall and early spring there were ducks, and in the winter, deer and bear. Sayer's men rigged a net in the river and caught fish.

The Ojibway to whom Sayer had given goods on credit came back from their fall hunt. They had 200 beaver skins "and paid their debts nobly." For a day or two they performed a solemn medicine ceremony. Then they divided into families and headed for winter lodges in the deep woods. By the end of December, snow was piled everywhere. Sayer wrote that the temperature had fallen to zero.

Sayer's post was rebuilt in the 1970s on the spot where it once stood. From Sayer's diary and traces in the the earth, archaeologists could guess how it looked.

Now the trader began to send his most trusted men to visit the Indians. They carried supplies of ammunition and brought back furs. Sayer feared that if he did not do this some of the families might go to other traders.

Indian men killed the animals and skinned them. Women scraped, stretched, and cured the hides. For this reason Ojibway women had much to say about what to do with the furs. Sayer wrote in his diary of his worry that some visiting employees of another trader "will poison the minds of the women by offering to sell cheaper than I do." Nevertheless, his storeroom began to fill with the soft, smelly skins of bear, beaver, wolf, marten, fisher, otter, mink, and muskrat. There were hides of deer and moose, too.

Otter

Spring came early that year. Warm days at the end of February brought up the sap in the maple trees. On March 1 Sayer wrote: "All the women went off to their sugar huts." These were bark wigwams built near groves of maple. The women, children, and older men of the tribe would camp there for a few weeks while they collected the sap from the trees and boiled it over open fires. When they had finished, they brought Sayer more than 175 pounds of maple sugar.

Muskrat

By then it was time to sort the furs into packs and make the canoes ready for the trip to Fort William. There Sayer expected to add up his profits and talk with his partners. While the furs went by ship to Montreal, the trader would be busy packing supplies and hiring men for his next winter in the woods. So the fur trade, like Indian life, followed a circle of seasons.

A maple sugar camp. The metal kettles brought by traders made boiling the sugar much easier.

Two Worlds Become One

Susan Johnston was a daughter of the Ojibway chief White Fisher. Her Ojibway name was Woman of the Green Prairie *(O-shaw-gus-co-day-way-qua).* When she was a girl, a young Irish trader named John Johnston asked the chief whether he could marry her. White Fisher told him to come back the next year. Johnston did. To prove he was sincere, he also agreed to wed according to white laws and customs. To be married before a priest, the bride had to become Christian. She did and was given the name Susan.

Johnston's business prospered. He hired other traders and had many posts around Lake Superior. Susan's influence among her own people helped him greatly. She was a tall, dignified woman who understood English but usually spoke Ojibway.

When John died, Susan ran the business. She was respected not only by Ojibway leaders but by white men as well. Her courage and common sense once kept war from breaking out while a treaty was being discussed.

Like Sayer, most successful traders married women from the tribe or band they traded with. It was a great help in business. Family ties meant much to Indian people. If a trader were new to the country, an Indian wife could interpret and teach him the language. She could tell him the customs of the people and which ones to trust. A few Indian wives became skilled traders themselves. When their husbands died, they continued the business.

For women, marrying a trader might mean wealth and influence. A trader's wife was respected and so was her family. But there was always the chance of his leaving. Many white men did not consider such marriages permanent. When a trader returned to the East, he often left his Indian wife with her own people. That is what John Sayer did.

Other traders and voyageurs stayed in the West with their wives and children. As years passed, these mixed or métis families gathered into communities. The daughters usually married métis men or sometimes white traders. A few of the sons became farmers. Some were hunters or guides. But most worked in the fur trade.

By the early 1800s some leading métis families had been in the trading business for more than three generations. They had close ties with other métis traders and Indian relatives. Their influence in the fur trade was strong. Among such families in Minnesota were the Renvilles, the Faribaults, the Beaulieus, and the Aitkens.

A métis family in their Red River cart

The largest métis community was in the Red River Valley. Some of the people lived in what is now Minnesota and North Dakota, but a larger group lived in Manitoba. They became famous buffalo hunters. They were also known for the two-wheeled carts that carried furs and hides from Canada and the Red River country across Minnesota to the Mississippi.

The Red River carts were made entirely of wood and were pulled by an ox or a pony. They screeched so loudly you could hear them for miles. Bumping and creaking across the prairie, they made deep ruts in the soft soil. For safety and for help in getting across rivers and mudholes, many drivers and carts traveled together.

A train of 100 or 200 carts might leave the métis town of Pembina on the Canadian border and travel two months before reaching St. Paul. The drivers—mostly men, but sometimes women—walked beside the carts and slept under them at night. The different routes they followed became known as the Red River trails. Between the 1830s and the 1860s, the métis and their carts helped to make the town of St. Paul into one of the most important fur markets in the country.

George Bonga

The Bongas were a métis family with a difference. Jean (Zhon) and Marie Bonga were black slaves. Their owner, a British army man, brought them to the English fort at Mackinac Island in 1782. Later he freed them. Jean bought a house on Mackinac and opened an inn.

Pierre Bonga, son of Jean and Marie, took a job with a trader headed for the Red River Valley. There he married an Ojibway woman and in time started trading on his own. His sons found work in the fur trade too. One of them was George.

George Bonga was more than six feet tall. People remembered his enormous strength and polished manners. His parents had sent him to school in Montreal, so he could speak French, English, and Ojibway. For this reason he often worked as an interpreter. Like his father, he married an Ojibway woman. Their descendants are still members of the Minnesota Chippewa (Ojibway) Tribe.

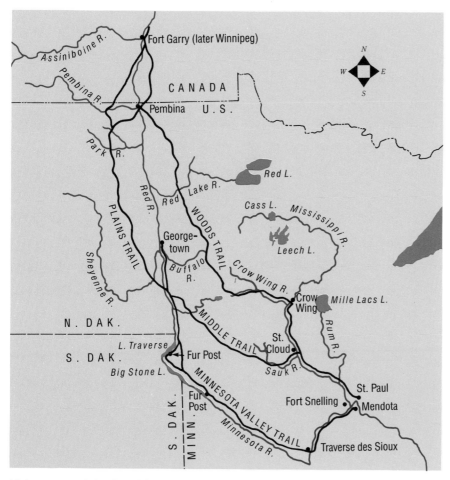

Main routes of the Red River trails

Unit III
The Land Changes Hands

Chapter 8
New Boundaries on the Prairies and in the Woods

The Americans Come

For nearly 150 years fur traders and European travelers had come and gone in the country we now call Minnesota. Most of them were not interested in changing the ways of Indian people or in owning the land. Some of them wrote reports and drew maps of what they found. The upper Mississippi valley and the area west of Lake Superior began to appear on charts of the world.

Far away in Europe, people gave names to the lakes and rivers and drew boundaries on paper. Different countries claimed Minnesota. At one time it appeared on maps as part of New France. Later it was divided between England and Spain, then among England, Spain, and a new country called the United States of America. Finally, the United States claimed all of it.

While the lines and colors on the maps kept changing, the woods and prairies stayed the same. They belonged to the people who lived there — the Dakota and the Ojibway. Indian people knew about the new boundaries. They also knew that thousands of Europeans had arrived on the shores of North America and built farms and cities. They had heard how tribes on the East Coast were pushed from their homes and how white settlers like Daniel Boone were moving west and taking even more Indian land. These things worried them deeply.

Not until 1805 did Indians see the first sign of change in Minnesota. In that year a young army officer named Zebulon Pike traveled with 20 soldiers up the Mississippi River. He camped on a flat, sandy island where the Minnesota River joins the Mississippi. There the Dakota bands met for a council with him. Pike told their leaders that he had been sent by the United States to find a good place for a fort. He gave gifts to the tribe. Then he asked whether they would let the Americans have some land. The Dakota thought it over and said a small amount of land would be all right.

Fourteen years passed before the fort was built. In the meantime the United States fought a war with England (the War of 1812), and the English sent some farmers to start a settlement on the Red River where Winnipeg now stands. The United States was suspicious about this Red River colony.

From the Mendota trading post overlooking Pike Island, artist J. C. Wild painted Fort Snelling in the early 1840s. Trader Henry Sibley owned the stone house at left front. Indian agency buildings stand along the edge of the bluff to the left of the fort.

Americans thought that England wanted to keep the rich fur trade of the upper Mississippi valley for itself. They felt American fur traders needed protection from the English. They also thought a fort was needed to keep peace among the Indians. Warfare between tribes made travel dangerous for traders and kept Indian hunters from gathering furs. So, in 1819, soldiers came to start building the fort.

Dakota Life in the Shadow of the Walls

There were five Dakota communities near Fort Snelling. Indian people still gathered for celebrations and trading where the rivers joined in the valley below the walls. Sometimes Ojibway came down the Mississippi from their own country to the north. They and the Dakota usually met in peace, but now and then old anger flared up. When there was trouble, the officers at the fort tried to punish those who started it.

A large American Fur Company trading post stood just across the river from Fort Snelling at a place that came to be called Mendota. To oversee the traders and to deal with Indian people, the government appointed men called Indian agents. Lawrence Taliaferro was the agent at Fort Snelling for the first 19 years (1820-1839). Next to the commander, he was the most important man there.

The buildings of the Indian agency stood near the fort. One was a council house, made of logs. Inside was a big room with a United States

The country around the western Great Lakes and the upper Mississippi River in 1820. The dotted lines show routes by which people reached Fort Snelling.

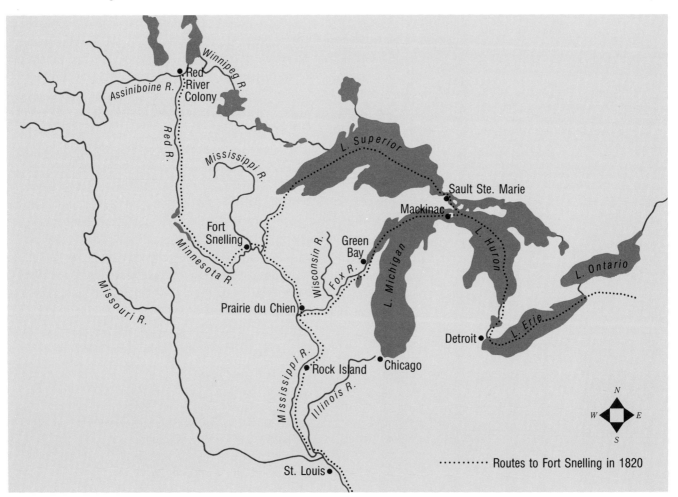

·········· Routes to Fort Snelling in 1820

flag in the center and gifts from the tribes hanging on the walls. Since the Indians liked to sit on the floor, the only furniture was a table and two or three chairs for the agent, his interpreter, and any other white visitors. Taliaferro kept no pen and ink in the room. He thought it was rude to write down things the Indians could not read.

Soldiers, traders, and agents were not the only people who came to the country of the Dakota. Some army men brought their wives and families as well as servants and a few black slaves. After 1823 steamboats made their way up the Mississippi, carrying visitors as well as supplies and mapmakers. In the 1830s missionaries who hoped to make the Dakota into Christians came and stayed. There were even a few settlers with homes on the government land around Fort Snelling. Most of these were people from the Red River colony who had traveled south looking for a better place to live.

As time passed, the Dakota saw many changes around the fort. The trees that had grown along the rivers were cut for firewood and for making fences and buildings. Beside the Falls of St. Anthony the soldiers built a mill, where they sawed logs into boards. They planted wheat on the flat land along the Minnesota River and built another mill to grind the wheat into flour. To the west of the fort were vegetable gardens. Buffalo had once roamed on the prairies there. Now they could not be found for hundreds of miles. Deer, bear, and other animals had also become scarce. It was harder

The Fort Snelling area in the 1830s. The shaded area is the land bought from the Dakota for the fort.

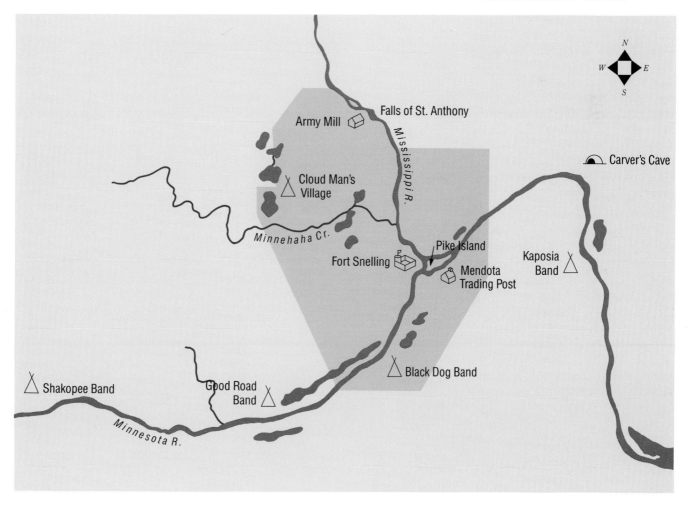

and harder for Indian people to find furs to buy the things they needed from traders. Sometimes they were tempted to kill army cattle pastured near the fort for food.

The Dakota had often lived through bad seasons when everyone went hungry. They were proud to bear it without complaining and to share what they had with each other. Now for the first time they knew what it was like to starve while others around them had plenty. They learned the feeling of being poor.

There was more sickness, too. The smallpox that killed thousands of Indian people in other parts of the country did not spread around Fort Snelling. There the army doctor vaccinated both Indian and white people. But no one had found a way to stop whooping cough yet. In the 1830s many Dakota children and some adults died from it. As life grew harder, alcoholism also spread. Traders were forbidden to sell liquor, but soldiers had it. The Dakota could always get it for a price.

Indian agent Taliaferro and his missionary friends never tired of telling the Dakota to become farmers. They had always grown corn in summer gardens, but planting whole fields was different. Some were willing to try. Others felt it was wrong to cut into the earth with a plow. Most Dakota just thought that farming was the way of white people, and they did not want to change. They wanted to be Dakota.

Lawrence Taliaferro (Tolliver) once wrote in his diary: "How to get rid of me at this Post seems now the main object of Tom, Dick, and Harry—so that those who may come after me can the more easily be bribed or threatened into silence and acquiesce in the plans on foot to cheat & destroy the Indians." He was not far wrong. The fur traders tried hard to get a different Indian agent at Fort Snelling. They never succeeded.

Taliaferro was fiercely honest. He was also stuffy and formal, sometimes quarrelsome, and always sure he was right. Like most white Americans of his time, he believed that Indians were much like children. His job, as he saw it, was to protect them from each other and from dishonest white men. He wanted to teach them to farm and to live like white people. For help in doing this, he looked to missionaries.

The Dakota placed the bodies of the dead on raised platforms. Artist Seth Eastman sketched these two mourners at a burial ground near Fort Snelling.

Treaties and More Treaties

Talk about treaties and land sales seemed never to stop. Indian people argued that land could not be owned or sold. The country was their home and it belonged to all who lived there, just as they belonged to it. The land held the graves of their ancestors and the sacred places of their religion. Other Indians had said the same things to whites for 200 years. But people whose ancestors were from Europe thought land was property to be bought and sold and fenced. The Dakota and Ojibway knew that if they did not sell their land, they would be forced to give it up anyway. The only question was what kind of bargain they could make.

The first loss came in 1837, when the government bought a big chunk of western Wisconsin from the Ojibway and all Dakota land east of the Mississippi. The tribes had not yet been paid when lumbermen rushed into the pine forests along the St. Croix River. The Indians heard the thud of axes and the crash of falling trees. They saw mills built and towns grow up at places like Taylors Falls and Stillwater.

Another town began to grow a few miles down the Mississippi from Fort Snelling. It was called Pig's Eye Landing, for a one-eyed man who opened a tavern there. Later settlers decided to name their town St. Paul, after the little log church built by a missionary. Across and down the river from St. Paul stood a much older settlement. It was the Dakota community

Cloud Man *(Ma-hpi-ya-wi-ća-sta)* was the first of the Dakota around Fort Snelling to try farming. He was a person who chose his own path. As a young man Cloud Man was brave in battle. But after killing six Ojibway, he decided to fight no more, and he never again went to war.

A few years later, when Cloud Man and some friends were hunting buffalo, a sudden blizzard hit. They dug hollows in the snow and curled up to keep from freezing. As he waited for the storm to pass, Cloud Man thought about farming. The next spring he moved his family to Lake Calhoun, where he planted corn and potatoes. Some of the Dakota sneered, but others joined him. Eight years later nearly five hundred people were living there and raising crops.

When some Ojibway shot a young man from the village, Cloud Man refused to lead his people in striking back. They chose another chief and killed many Ojibway. But then they knew their enemies would return. So they left their farms and moved to a safer place in the Minnesota Valley.

In the 1830s visiting artist George Catlin sketched these cattle grazing near Cloud Man's village at Lake Calhoun.

of Kaposia *(Kah-po-źa)*. The chief there was Little Crow *(Kan-ghi-ći-śti-na)*. He and his people anxiously watched the changes on the east side of the Mississippi. Soon, they knew, they would have to leave.

They were right. Within ten years there was talk of another treaty, and in 1851 the Dakota were called together to discuss selling all their Minnesota land. After much arguing, it became clear to the Dakota leaders that they would have to give up their homeland. Some of their people were starving. The traders, to whom the Dakota owed money, said they would give no more credit. Government officials threatened to hold back horses and food they had promised to the tribe. So the Dakota signed two treaties, one for the western Minnesota bands at Traverse des Sioux and one near the trading post of Mendota for those farther east. In return for most of southern Minnesota, they got 12½ cents an acre and a small reservation along the Minnesota River. By 1855, the Ojibway bands had also signed treaties selling most of their land.

Seth Eastman made this sketch of the Dakota town of Kaposia in the 1840s. A missionary's house and garden are at left. There is a Dakota cemetery on the hill above.

Life in the Fort

Colonel Josiah Snelling was no spit-and-polish officer, but his troops respected him. He designed the fort, oversaw the long job of building it, and commanded it for nearly eight years (1820-1827). Everyone agreed that he deserved to have it named for him. When sober, Snelling was a tough but fair-minded man. When he drank (as most army officers did), he had a terrible temper. Because his bald head with its fringe of reddish hair reminded the men at the fort of a ruffed grouse, they called him "the Prairie Chicken"—but not when he could hear them.

Fort Snelling no longer stood in Indian country. For 30 years its solid walls had told the Dakota that another nation held power over them. For 30 years it had been an island of white American life and customs. It had never been attacked, and its soldiers had fought no battles. Their worst enemies had been loneliness, boredom, bitter cold, and hard work.

Each winter when the river froze and boats could no longer come up the Mississippi, the fort was cut off from the outside world. The nearest settlement was at Prairie du Chien (doo Sheen), more than two hundred miles away. Letters and army orders had to be carried on foot or by dogsled on dangerous ice along the river. In the winter of 1826, no mail got through for five months.

Keeping the fort warm during Minnesota winters was a never-ending job. The wood needed for the fireplaces for one winter could make a pile four feet high, four feet wide, and two miles long. The soldiers had to chop and haul all of it. They also had to cut timber and saw boards for buildings and fences, quarry limestone for walls, plow, plant, and hoe fields and gardens, make hay for the cattle and horses, unload supplies from boats and haul them up the hill to the fort, grind flour in the gristmill, and shovel snow in winter. They often felt more like farmers or lumberjacks than soldiers.

Soldiers practiced pulling light cannons with horses on the prairie west of Fort Snelling in 1855.

Ordinary soldiers everywhere had hard lives in the early 1800s. Pay was poor, and their days were ruled by the drum from dawn to dark. Even at a lonely post like Fort Snelling, where about three hundred people lived close together, the difference between officers and men was great. A soldier could not speak to an officer until spoken to. Rules were strict and punishment was fierce. For being drunk, sloppy, or disrespectful to an officer, a man could be thrown in the guardhouse. There he might wear a ball and chain and eat only bread and water. For disobeying orders or running away he might be sentenced to years of hard labor.

A private's pay was not enough to support a family. Soldiers' wives lived at the fort only if they could get jobs as army laundresses or as servants to officers' families. For this reason, most of the laundresses hired for work at the fort were married women. Those who were not married lived in a log building on the riverbank below the walls.

Each day of army life was much like another, but it was not always dull. Hunting and fishing were favorite sports for officers and soldiers who had a few free hours. Many officers kept hunting dogs, and most had horses. In the summer, steamboats, visitors, and sightseeing trips helped keep things lively.

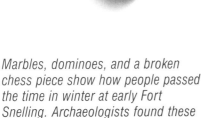

Marbles, dominoes, and a broken chess piece show how people passed the time in winter at early Fort Snelling. Archaeologists found these objects there.

Abigail Hunt Snelling was the daughter, sister, wife, and mother of army officers. She was 22 years old and nine months pregnant when she and Josiah arrived at the site of Fort Snelling in 1820. Two weeks later she had a baby girl who lived only a few months.

A strong, active, determined woman, Abigail Snelling held parties, entertained visitors to the fort, and studied French. She insisted on a school for the children. She was kind to several unlucky families from the Red River colony and adopted an orphaned boy whose parents had died on the trip. Her example made the fort a place where homes, families, and polite ways were never quite forgotten. People remembered her slender figure, her flashing dark eyes, and her long black hair. She was an expert horseback rider and loved to go for a gallop on the prairies behind the fort.

Time passed more slowly in winter. The fort had a small library, and newspapers from the East were saved and passed around. Officers' wives put on parties and balls. The soldiers and their families had country-style dances in the barracks. When there were enough talented people, plays and concerts were performed. Even with these amusements, everyone agreed that the long winter days and nights saw too much gambling, drinking, gossiping, and quarreling.

For children, life at the fort was full of excitement. Eight-year-old Henry Snelling remembered celebrating the Fourth of July in 1827 with other young boys from the fort. They collected toy guns and gunpowder, some cake and cookies, ale to drink, and four or five man-sized cigars. With these they went to their hideout in a cave below the fort. They had a great time until they smoked the cigars and got violently sick. Another time young Snelling fell into the river and nearly drowned. When a passing soldier fished him out, he insisted that a giant catfish had pulled him in. Girls had less freedom and more rules, but they, too, enjoyed family picnics and trips to places like Carver's Cave and the Falls of St. Anthony.

Paul Kane, from the Red River colony, painted these Dakota women holding a solemn ceremonial dance in the valley below Fort Snelling.

Worlds Apart

Nearly everyone who lived at the fort had an uneasy sense of being surrounded by an unfamiliar world. The miles of prairie stretching to the west and the silent river bluffs to the east seemed strange and empty to people who were used to farms, fences, roads, and towns. They wrote to friends in the East of the "savage wilderness" around them. Some thought it was beautiful. Others were afraid.

They felt much the same about Indians. From the fort they could almost always see the smoke of campfires and the pointed tops of a few tipis. Many Dakota and some Ojibway came and went from the Indian agency outside the main gate. Often they visited inside the walls. When they gathered in the valley below for games or ceremonies, their singing and drumming could be heard day and night. Some people at the fort were fascinated, but others found it strange and upsetting.

One officer with a great interest in Indian ways was Seth Eastman. He was an artist, and the pictures he sketched with his pencil and paintbrush are some of the best "snapshots" ever made of Dakota life. Eastman first came to the fort in 1829 as a young lieutenant. He fell in love with a Dakota woman, and they had a child. When he was moved to another post, he left her behind. Years later he returned to the fort as a senior officer. This time he brought with him a white wife named Mary and a family.

Nancy Eastman *(Wa-kan-tan-ka-win* or Great Spirit Woman) was a daughter of two worlds. Her mother was a Dakota named Stands Like a Spirit *(Wa-kan-ina-jin-win).* Her father was the artist and soldier Seth Eastman.

Nancy was cared for by her Dakota grandmother, who did not want the child to learn the ways of white people. When Nancy was 17, she fell in love and decided to elope.

In running away, she was tricked by a friend of the young man she loved. The friend, Many Lightnings *(Wa-kan-hdi-o-ta),* also admired Nancy. When he learned of her plan, he managed to take the place of her lover. In the dark she did not discover that she had gone with the wrong man until it was too late. In spite of his trick, she became the devoted wife of Many Lightnings, and they had five children. Soon after the last one was born, Nancy fell ill. As she was dying, she asked the mother of Many Lightnings to raise the baby boy.

A short time later, in 1862, Many Lightnings joined his people in war against the Americans. He was captured and sent to prison. There he became a Christian and borrowed the name Jacob Eastman from Nancy's family. After he was released, Jacob searched for his children, who had been scattered during the war. He found his mother and his youngest son in Canada. Bringing them back, he named the boy Charles Alexander Eastman. Charles, the son of Nancy and Many Lightnings, went to college in the East and became a doctor. Later he returned to his people and wrote books about growing up among the Dakota.

Mary Eastman, like her husband, made many Dakota friends. She wrote down the stories they told her. She was a warmhearted person, and the suffering she saw among the Dakota women moved her deeply. "Frequently," she wrote, "we have heard of whole families perishing during severely cold weather. The father absent on a winter's hunt, the mother could not leave her children to apply to the fort for assistance, even had she strength left to reach there. The frozen bodies would be found in the lodge."

Trying to find a reason for such horrors, Mary blamed the Dakota way of life. In a book she wrote later, she told of "the immense good that might be accomplished among these tribes by schools, which should open the minds of the young to the light of reason and Christianity." Like most Americans of her time, she was sure that Indians were a "doomed race" and that the only way to save them was to make them like white people.

Books like hers helped missionaries who were working to have Indians treated fairly. But her words also made it easy for Americans to picture Fort Snelling as a first step toward bringing the good things of their own civilization to a wild country. Most white people preferred to see it that way. They did not like to think of themselves as invaders taking homes away from others.

Artist Frank Mayer made these sketches of Nancy Eastman along with other drawings in his notebook.

Chapter 9
The New Minnesotans

Land for Many People

White Americans thought they were right to take the prairies and forests of Minnesota from Indian people. Many felt they were bringing the Indians a better way of life—one with less fear and suffering and hunger. They did not ask whether the Indians wanted change. Americans also thought they could put the land to better use. Indian people shaped their lives to the natural world, leaving plants and animals alone unless they were needed for food and clothing. Living this way meant that much land supported only a few people. Americans knew that if they cut the trees and plowed the prairies, they could feed many more on the rich fields of southern Minnesota.

Thousands of people were waiting for that land. There were those who lived on rocky farms in New England and other eastern states. They dreamed of getting a new start in the West. And there were people in countries like Germany and Sweden and Ireland who had no land at all. They were willing to leave friends and country to make the long, risky trip to a strange place—if it meant they could have a farm for themselves and their children. To people already living in towns like Stillwater and St. Paul, new settlers meant more business and more money for all of Minnesota.

Turning woods and grassland into farms, however, was not easy. A farm is owned by someone. It is measured in acres and has boundaries. After the government signed a treaty for a stretch of country, it had to divide the land up by measuring and marking. This is called surveying. When the sections were sold a record had to be kept of where they were and who owned them. It all took time and money.

St. Paul was the last good landing place for steamboats coming up the Mississippi. It became Minnesota's capital in 1849 and grew to the town shown here by 1856.

Organizing a Government

When the United States bought the first big piece of Minnesota in 1837, a few people rushed right in. They cut timber and staked out farms on land that had not been surveyed, knowing they could buy it later. But there was much land to be surveyed, and the government was not in a hurry.

Settlers needed other government services too—roads, post offices, schools, courts, and police. The way to get services was to organize and demand them. So the new Minnesotans did. In 1848 a group of 61 men met in Stillwater and agreed to send a representative to Washington. He would ask Congress to make Minnesota a legal territory, with a governor, a legislature, and courts of its own. They chose Henry H. Sibley, who ran the American Fur Company's trading post at Mendota. Nearly everyone knew and trusted him, and he had many friends in the government in Washington.

Sibley was successful. The next year, in 1849, Minnesota became a territory. Now the citizens had the right to vote for a legislature and to send someone to Congress. They would have courts and a person in Washington to lobby for roads, mail service, surveying, and new treaties. In their first regular election, Minnesotans again chose Henry Sibley as their representative. The territory's other important officer was a governor appointed by the president. The man the president chose was a young Pennsylvania politician named Alexander Ramsey.

Henry H. Sibley has been called "the Princely Pioneer." He was a handsome man with education and polished manners. His father was chief justice of the Michigan Supreme Court. His great-grandfather had been a hero of the American Revolution. Sibley became a fur trader instead of a banker because he wanted adventure and liked the outdoors. At Mendota he built a stately stone house where he had many guests. He often went on long hunting trips with the Dakota, who called him "Walker in the Pines."

Sibley represented Minnesota Territory in Congress for two terms (1849-1853). Later he helped write the state constitution. The voters chose him to be their first state governor. When the Dakota War broke out in 1862, they turned again to Sibley. He led an army against the Indians he had lived and worked with for many years.

A Territory Built on Rivers

With his wife, Anna, and their baby son, Governor Ramsey traveled up the Mississippi River by steamboat in May 1849. The boat reached St. Paul before dawn and quietly pulled to shore. While the other passengers slept, Ramsey got off and walked around the town. Climbing the steep hill from the river, he found a cluster of log and board buildings, many without paint and some still unfinished. "There was hardly the suspicion of a street," he recalled, "but the houses were scattered about here and there as suited the fancy." Ramsey may also have noticed a few stores, two hotels, a school, a church, a newspaper office, and half a dozen taverns. There were no sidewalks or lawns or shade trees.

Perched high on its bluff, the little town seemed to watch the river. Ramsey would soon find that all Minnesota's settlements were close to rivers. Whether it was the Mississippi, the St. Croix, or the Minnesota, the river was a link to the outside world—to friends, old homes, news, and markets. When a steamboat came within sight of a town, its captain blew the whistle or fired a gun. The people gathered at the bank, or levee, to see who was coming. They helped unload boxes and bales of goods and asked questions about what had been happening "out east." The slow-moving paddle-wheelers carried groceries, coal, cloth, candles, paper, furniture, tools, machinery, cows, chickens, and horses. Most important of all were the letters and newspapers.

Alexander Ramsey was a blunt, practical man. He disliked fuss and formality. Because of this his political friends called him "Bluff Alec." His enemies sometimes called him "the old coon." They meant he was shrewd and hard to catch, like a raccoon that ate farmers' chickens.

On his first walk through St. Paul, no one knew who Ramsey was. He asked a young boy about one of the unfinished houses he saw. The boy answered, "They're getting it ready for the governor." Ramsey could see that it would not be done for a while. So he accepted Henry Sibley's invitation to stay at Mendota. The two men became firm friends, although they were often on opposite sides in politics.

Ramsey was elected second governor of the state in 1860. A year later, while he was in Washington, war started in the South. Hurrying to the White House, he told President Abraham Lincoln of Minnesota's support. He was the first to offer troops to fight for the Union. Later Ramsey became a U.S. senator.

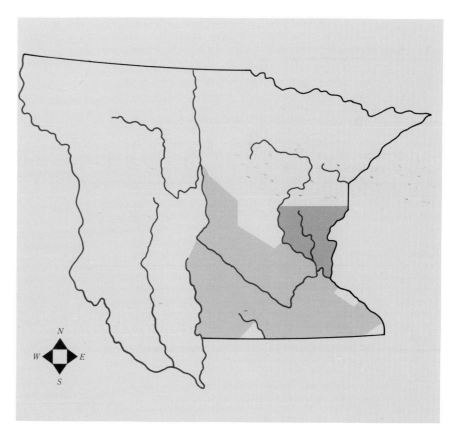

Minnesota Territory reached west to the Missouri River and took in parts of what are now North and South Dakota. The darker area was the only part of Minnesota open to white settlers in 1849. The lighter area was opened by treaties with the Dakota Indians in 1851.

The river also carried things away. On the return to St. Louis, steamboats were loaded with furs and skins gathered by the Dakota and Ojibway or brought by carts over the Red River trails. Each year, too, thousands of logs from the pine forests of Wisconsin and Minnesota floated down rivers like the St. Croix and the Rum. At places like Stillwater they were sorted and tied into rafts to be floated or towed down the Mississippi.

Sawmills in towns farther south made the logs into lumber. All across prairie states like Illinois and Iowa, barns and fences and houses were being built with pine boards from the north. There were already a few sawmills in Minnesota, too. The best place for these was at the Falls of St. Anthony, as the Fort Snelling soldiers had discovered. There the power of the falling water turned large wheels called turbines. These were attached by belts and pulleys to rows of saws and other machines. Beside the mills the village of St. Anthony grew on the east bank of the Mississippi.

The People Who Came

The people who built the sawmills and cut the pine trees had worked in the lumber industry before. Many came from the timber states of Maine and New Hampshire. Some were from other parts of New England, from New York, or, like Governor Ramsey, from Pennsylvania. A number were from Canada. Their ancestors had come from England or Scotland or northern Ireland. They brought to Minnesota strong feelings about democracy, laws, schools, and

Logs and lumber mills at the Falls of St. Anthony in the 1850s

churches. These people were the leaders in the towns of the new territory. Because of them, Minnesota was sometimes called "the New England of the West."

The new governor, like others, wanted to see the territory grow. In his first speech to the Minnesota legislature he called for a treaty to buy the rich farming country west of the Mississippi. Two years later he was one of the officials who bargained with the Dakota for their land.

Until that time there had not been many farms in the territory, but after 1851 hundreds and then thousands of new farmers came each year. Many were from the eastern United States, but before long others began to join them. There were families from southern Ireland who had come to escape the terrible famines in that country. There were many Germans and people from Sweden and Norway.

Boatload after boatload of immigrants landed in the towns along the rivers and spread out into the country beyond. Soon there were whole communities where hardly anyone spoke English. Sometimes the names of places told where people had come from. New Ulm, Vasa, New Prague, St. Patrick, Scandia, Heidelberg, Dumfries, and many other names called to mind homelands far away. The immigrants of the 1850s were only the first of many thousands more. Before long Minnesota was not only a midwestern New England. It was also a "New Sweden," a "New Norway," and a "New Germany."

Joseph Rolette was one of Minnesota Territory's lawmakers. Like many others in the new legislature, he was a frontiersman. His father had been a fur trader. His mother was the daughter, granddaughter, and great-granddaughter of fur traders. He represented the métis settlement of Pembina.

Each winter Joe went to St. Paul by dogsled. People knew him for his tall tales, practical jokes, colorful costumes, and hearty backwoods friendliness. No one was surprised when he played a joke on the legislature that made a difference in Minnesota's history.

A bill had been passed to move the capital of the territory from St. Paul to St. Peter. Joe did not like it. So he took the official copy of the law and hid out. For a week he drank and played poker with his friends. The other lawmakers fumed. When it was too late to get the bill signed into law, he came back. Minnesota's capital stayed in St. Paul.

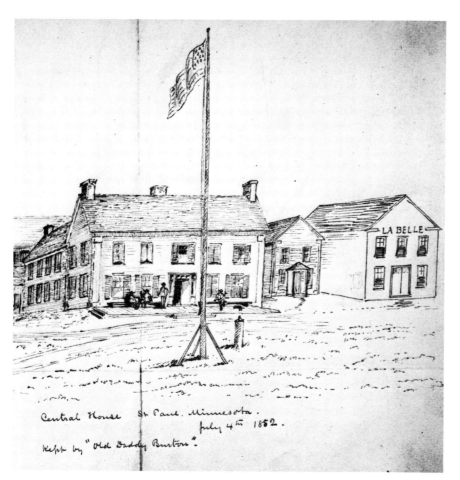

Central House St. Paul. Minnesota.
July 4th 1852.
Kept by "Old Daddy Burton".

The first legislature met in this hotel next to the La Belle Saloon.

Life in the Territory

People often think of all pioneers as farmers who came in covered wagons and built log cabins. Some were, but the kind of life that immigrants found depended on what they worked at and where they settled. Josef Kaplan left Bohemia (now Czechoslovakia) with his wife Barbara in 1856. They made the six-week voyage across the Atlantic in a sailing ship to Quebec, Canada. From there they traveled by boat and train to Freeport, Illinois, where some Czech friends had settled. On January 1, 1857, Josef wrote a letter to neighbors and relatives back home:

"You are no doubt surprised, dear friends, at the address: Owatonna. That is our nearest town, founded two years ago.

"I promised to tell you about our journey from Freeport to Minnesota across parts of Iowa and Wisconsin to the northwest. It was quite a hard trip, but there's no help for it.

"Every morning at eight o'clock we started out and rode till three or four o'clock in the afternoon. Then we made camp somewhere near a brook, let the stock out to pasture on grass which on the American prairies grows hip high, and then proceeded to cook our food. After that the cattle were tied to the wagons for the night and we went to sleep in the wagons.

"You are probably thinking about the discomfort and perhaps the danger. As for the first, even a millionaire must endure it here if he wants to travel where there are no railroads. As for the second, a small company

Covered wagons like the one the Kaplans traveled in are shown above on the main street of Owatonna in the early 1860s. The sketch at left is from a photograph of the log cabin that Josef Kaplan built on his farm.

doesn't usually undertake such a journey, and we were ten families—three Czech and the rest German and French.

"On the way we had to cross the great Mississippi; the river is a good half hour's journey wide. And so we finally reached the place I mentioned above. Here we selected a section of government land, which is an area a mile square. Everyone at least 21 years old is allowed to buy one quarter section. The first task is to erect a building on it as quickly as possible, no matter how, and to make hay for the cattle. After building, one notifies the land office which quarter section he has taken and pays $1.50 per acre."

A year later Josef wrote: "We lack nothing now and are looking for a better future. But, my friends, to bring virgin soil, ages untouched, to its first harvest gives one hard calluses, and much sweat flows over one's brow before he can enjoy its produce. As for the women, they have it worse, but when they must bear any misfortune here, they do it without lamentation."

The newcomers who settled in Minnesota's early towns found life quite different from that of frontier farmers. Joseph Ullmann, a St. Paul storekeeper, had come from the province of Alsace, on the border between France and Germany. After a few years in New Orleans and St. Louis, he moved to St. Paul in 1855. His wife, Amelia, and their baby son followed a short time later by steamboat.

This portrait of Amelia Ullmann was painted a short time after she came to St. Paul. The Ullmanns were among German-Jewish pioneers who formed Minnesota's first synagogue in 1856.

St. Paul was a raw boom town, crowded with immigrants. Housing was so scarce that the little family had to stay in a single small hotel room through the summer. Finally they found an apartment. Amelia recalled the misery of being a careful homemaker and devoted mother when she was still a stranger in the frontier town: "Every drop of water used had to be carried across the prairie from a well in a livery stable back of the American hotel. To get this it was necessary to crowd in among drivers and rough men from the prairies. My child was ill much of the time from lack of proper nourishment, for good, wholesome food was difficult to obtain. Fresh vegetables and fruits were unknown."

Even fresh meat and milk were luxuries for most of the newcomers in town. The usual food for all three meals was bacon, potatoes, and tea. On special occasions, like Christmas dinner, there might be fresh venison, wild goose or duck, and cranberries, which grew wild in Minnesota.

The Ullmans found their apartment alive with bedbugs. Then they learned that five people in the house had died from cholera the year before. So they moved to a tiny room behind Joseph's store.

Pioneer storekeepers did not spend all their time keeping books or serving customers. They had to lay in a large stock of goods before the river froze in early winter. After that St. Paul was cut off from the rest of the world until the ice broke in April or May. By then the shelves would be bare. A good businessman had to go to St. Louis in late winter to order goods for shipment on the first steamboat in the spring.

The American Hotel in 1858

People who were hardy enough could travel on the winter mail coach that ran each week between St. Paul and the nearest towns down the Mississippi. The "coach" was an open wagon on runners, pulled by a team of horses. Every 15 miles the horses, panting and worn out from the hard pull, had to be changed. Each night the coach stopped at a station. This was a small log building with a loft full of hay for the passengers to sleep on.

In March 1857, as Joseph was getting ready to leave, Amelia announced that she, too, was going. He was horrified. "It is impossible for a woman to make such a trip," he said. He offered to buy her a new fur cloak if she would stay home. But Amelia only answered, "I am younger than you and equally as strong." There the argument ended.

The two dressed in their warmest clothes and wrapped themselves in a small mountain of furs and blankets. They packed a bag with wine, cold chicken, and other things to eat along the way. Two hours after they started, snow began to fall. Next morning when they left the first station, the road was buried. The horses plowed along, almost up to their bellies in snow. Suddenly the team sank nearly out of sight in a drift. Frightened and struggling wildly, the horses turned the sled over. Driver, passengers, and baggage were all dumped into the snow. The men worked for more than an hour to dig out the horses and get the sled loaded again. In spite of such mishaps, the travelers made it through.

These steamboats crowded the St. Paul levee in 1858.

A Country
of Many Promises

Travel by steamboat in the summer was much easier, especially for people who could afford first-class cabins on the upper deck. It was so pleasant that some made the trip to St. Paul just to enjoy themselves and see the scenery along the river. But most of the people who rode on steamboats were not tourists. Many travelers, both rich and poor, were brought by jobs or business. On the lower deck were crowds of immigrants.

Some people came to Minnesota in search of better health. They were told that the cold, dry winters and pure air could cure sickness. One who came was William W. Mayo, a young doctor from Indiana. Every summer he had spells of weakness. First he was hot, then he shook with cold. His illness was probably malaria. Like others, Dr. Mayo moved to Minnesota hoping that the climate would help him. It did.

Young men often looked to the West for a chance to work or start a new life. A few unmarried women came, too. Most of them were teachers or servants. There were not many other ways then for a woman to make a living by herself. In 1847 Harriet Bishop, who lived in New York state, heard that St. Paul needed teachers. She came and opened the town's first school.

In 1856 an 18-year-old Canadian named James J. Hill rode up the river on a steamboat. By the time he got off he had been hired as a clerk by one of the steamboat men. His job was to see that freight to St. Paul was unloaded and reached the right people. "I like this country very well and I

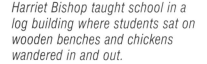

Harriet Bishop taught school in a log building where students sat on wooden benches and chickens wandered in and out.

think I shall like it better the longer I live here," he soon wrote to his grandmother. "My salary is twice as much as I could get in Canada and work is easy, all done in an office."

The dream of building a city drew a young Irish-American named Ignatius Donnelly to Minnesota. He and his partner bought land and divided it into streets and lots. They sold the lots to people in the East, telling them that the city of Nininger would soon stand there. Donnelly built a home and tried to get others to move to Nininger. For a while the scheme seemed to work. Then hard times came. The price of land fell, and the people who had bought lots found that they were worth almost nothing. Those already living in Nininger began to leave. Buildings were torn down or moved to the nearby town of Hastings. At last Donnelly's house was the only one left. Instead of being rich, as he had hoped, he was deeply in debt. To pay his debts, he planted the city lots with wheat.

In spite of such disappointments, it was a time of hope and promise. Everyone dreamed of making a fortune. Getting rich seemed a natural part of founding a new state and opening a great future to one's grandchildren and great-grandchildren. In the 1850s people never stopped talking about buying and selling land and planning towns and building railroads. Thousands of newcomers poured into Minnesota. There were 6,000 white people in 1850. Just ten years later there were 30 times that many. Most of them were young. All were in a hurry.

Dr. William Mayo and his two sons founded the famous Mayo Clinic in Rochester.

The first-class passenger cabin of the steamboat Milwaukee, *which served St. Paul in the 1850s*

In 1854 the first railroad train reached the Mississippi River at Rock Island, Illinois. Next year the first steamboats puffed their way into Lake Superior through the new Soo Canal. The government sent a team of army men to look for the best railroad route between St. Paul and the West Coast. In 1858 more than a thousand boatloads of goods and people reached St. Paul. That year Minnesota became a state.

Businessmen and politicians were sure that before long it would be the greatest state in the nation. They pictured ocean ships sailing to the end of Lake Superior. From there trains would take freight and people to the Pacific Ocean. Never mind the miles in between! Never mind that herds of buffalo still roamed the western country! Never mind that the plains and mountains belonged to Indian people! Americans had big dreams. The sooner farms and cities and railroads were built, the sooner those dreams would come true.

Ignatius Donnelly gave up promoting cities and went into politics. Later he became a voice for Minnesota's farmers and workers.

Young James Hill stayed in the freight business and later built railroads.

EMIGRATION

UP THE MISSISSIPPI RIVER.

The attention of Emigrants and the Public generally, is called to the now rapidly improving

TERRITORY OF MINNESOTA,

Containing a population of 150,000, and goes into the Union as a State during the present year. According to an act of Congress passed last February, the State is munificently endowed with Lands for Public Schools and State Universities, also granting five per cent. on all sales of U. S. Lands for Internal Improvements. On the 3d March, 1857, grants of Land from Congress was made to the leading Trunk Railroads in Minnesota, so that in a short time the trip from New Orleans to any part of the State will be made in from two and a half to three days. The

CITY OF NININGER,

Situated on the Mississippi River, 35 miles below St. Paul, is now a prominent point for a large Commercial Town, being backed by an extensive Agricultural, Grazing and Farming Country; has fine streams in the interior, well adapted for Milling in all its branches; and Manufacturing **WATER POWER** to any extent.

Mr. JOHN NININGER, (a Gentleman of large means, ideas and liberality, speaking the various languages,) is the principal Proprietor of **Nininger**. He laid it out on such principles as to encourage all **MECHANICS**, Merchants, or Professions of all kinds, on the same equality and footing; the consequence is, the place has gone ahead with such rapidity that it is now an established City, and will annually double in population for years to come.

Persons arriving by Ship or otherwise, can be transferred without expense to Steamers going to Saint Louis; or stop at Cairo, and take Railroad to Dunleith (on the Mississippi). Steamboats leave Saint Louis and Dunleith daily for **NININGER**, and make the trip from Dunleith in **36 to 48 hours.**

Posters like this were sent to eastern states to bring more people to Minnesota and to build up its towns and cities.

Chapter 10
War in the South

People Divided

While the new Minnesotans were hustling and scheming to build a state, the United States was slowly drawing to the edge of civil war. There were many deep divisions between the North and South, but the greatest was the question of slavery. Each time a new state was created in the West, the debate over whether it would be slave or free grew more bitter.

Most of Minnesota's people had never owned slaves and never wanted to. So when their representatives met to write a constitution that would set forth the rules and principles for governing the new state, no one said slavery should be allowed. But there was sharp disagreement about some related questions. How should free black people be treated? Should they be citizens? Should they vote? Over these questions Minnesotans at the constitutional convention shouted and had fistfights and walked out. They almost failed to agree on a constitution.

Another question raised deep feelings and threats of violence: Should southern visitors to Minnesota be allowed to bring slaves with them? The Mississippi River was like a highway between Minnesota and the cotton plantations of the South. Hundreds of steamboats traveled along it, carrying passengers in comfort and style. By the end of the 1850s, wealthy southerners often came north for the summer. Hotels in St. Anthony and Minneapolis welcomed them. To the struggling frontier communities they brought business and money—and also a few black slaves.

Most people saw no great harm in this. "We don't believe in slavery," wrote one newspaper editor, "and we rejoice that Minnesota is a free state, but when people come up here from the South, and, relying upon the honor and good faith of our people, bring along with them their servants, we don't think it looks well for us to interfere."

Howard Pyle caught the noise, confusion, and shock of a Civil War battle in this painting of Minnesota troops at Nashville in 1864.

Freedom
for Eliza Winston

One of these "servants" was a young woman named Eliza Winston. She belonged to Richard E. Christmas, a well-to-do Mississippi plantation owner. Her duties were to care for the Christmas baby and to wait on Mrs. Christmas, who was unwell. When the family came to Minnesota in the summer of 1860, they brought Eliza with them.

Eliza liked her mistress, who treated her kindly. Still she wanted freedom. She had been married to a free black man, but he died before he could save enough money to pay her owner. So Eliza's hope for freedom had ended sadly—but not her desire for it.

When Eliza reached Minnesota, she knew she was in a free state and could legally walk away from her master. But where would she go? How would she live? Would anyone help her? These questions were answered when she met Emily Grey. Emily and her husband Ralph were free black people who lived in Minneapolis. They were friends of the antislavery leader Frederick Douglass, and they were deeply committed to seeking freedom for all slaves. They knew white people in Minnesota who would help Eliza, too.

Before Eliza could get away from the hotel where the Christmases were staying, the family moved to a house in the country on Lake Harriet. The Greys feared Eliza would be kept a prisoner there until she could be taken back to the South. With their white friends, they complained to a

St. Anthony and Minneapolis, with their scenic waterfall, were favorite summer resorts for southern slave owners in the 1850s.

Minneapolis judge that the woman was being held a slave against the law of Minnesota. The sheriff went to rescue her, along with several antislavery people. The Christmas family tried to hide Eliza, but when the sheriff found her they did not resist.

Next day the whole town was excited. Antislavery people were joyful because the law had been enforced. Others claimed that Eliza had been kidnapped and that the home of the Christmas family had been invaded. A court hearing was held, and a threatening crowd gathered outside the door. There was talk of making Eliza return to her owner. But Christmas knew the law, and he told Eliza she was free to go. The judge agreed.

Afraid the proslavery people might harm Eliza, her friends quickly hid her. That night a mob surrounded the house where people thought she was staying. They threw stones through the windows, and some men tried to get in. They were frightened away when a pistol went off inside the house. Others broke into the Grey home to search for Eliza, but she was not there. Before many days she was sent safely to Canada.

Minnesota newspapers soon took sides on the case of Eliza Winston. In St. Paul the *Pioneer and Democrat* described antislavery people as "radical nigger stealers." In St. Anthony the *Weekly Express* reported that rich southerners were leaving town with their slaves and added angrily: "St. Anthony has lost thousands of dollars by this infamous transaction." Even in a free state, it was still risky to work openly against slavery.

This advertisement appeared in a St. Paul newspaper in the summer of 1860. The Christmas family and their servants stayed at the Winslow House before moving to Lake Harriet.

"The Cause Is So Just"

But times were changing fast. Only four months after Eliza Winston was freed, Abraham Lincoln became president. The southern states started to withdraw from the Union, and by the spring of 1861 the Civil War had begun. Minnesota, just three years old, was the first state to offer troops to fight for the North.

Edward Davis had been surveying for a new railroad when the news of war came. From St. Paul he wrote to his father in New York: "There is very great excitement here, and ten regiments could easily be raised in this state within a week. Flags are flying in all directions and rosettes, Red, White and Blue, are worn by men and women. As for business, it is at a standstill. I have enlisted for 3 months."

Not everyone thought separation of the states was worth a war. Even fewer believed in fighting to end slavery. Friends, neighbors, and families like that of Charles Shedd were divided. Shedd was a minister at Mantorville, Minnesota. His son Cornelius was working in Alabama. In May 1861, Cornelius wrote to his sister Maria, who had urged him to come to Minnesota. He told her that he liked the South and that forcing the southern states to stay in the Union would be like forcing the American colonies to stay under England. He asked: "Have your people counted the cost of subduing the South?" At almost the same time, Shedd's other son, Richmond, was headed for St. Paul to join the Second Minnesota Regiment. Three years and many battles later, Richmond Shedd died in Tennessee.

Dred and Harriet Scott were slaves, brought to Fort Snelling by their owners. In 1836 they were married, and Harriet's owner, Lawrence Taliaferro, sold her to Dred Scott's owner, Dr. John Emerson. Fort Snelling was in free territory. Slavery was illegal, but there were no courts and no one tried to enforce the law. When Dr. Emerson returned to the slave state of Missouri, he took Dred and Harriet with him.

Years later the Scotts sued in the courts. They claimed that because they had been taken to live in a free territory, they were free. The U.S. Supreme Court did not agree. In a famous decision in 1857, the court ruled that slaves taken to free territory were still "property."

Free states did not admit that black people could be property. So Eliza Winston could become free while she was in Minnesota. But under the court's ruling in the Dred Scott case, she would still be a slave if she went back to Mississippi with the Christmas family.

During the four years of the Civil War, Minnesota sent 25,000 men to fight the South. More than six hundred were killed in battle, and twice that number died of disease in army camps. The soldiers wrote thousands of letters to families and friends in Minnesota. The letters that have been saved tell firsthand the story of a nation at war with itself.

Madison Bowler and Lizzie Caleff had been engaged for nearly a year. In April 1861, Madison wrote Lizzie that he had enlisted. "So many of my friends are going and the cause is so just, that I cannot resist." He reminded her that she had said: "Go, if you think it your duty."

It was fall when Madison left Fort Snelling for Kentucky with the Third Minnesota Regiment. In December Lizzie wrote from her home near Hastings: "If you only knew my feelings when I get in some lone corner and sit down to think, and hear the wind whistle through the cracks and the snow blow round the corners. Shall you ever return to bless me with your smile?" A few days later she asked: "Why is it you do not write? I hope sickness is not the reason. I suppose you often feel lonely, but you have something exciting all the time. You never can imagine how lonely I feel when I think of you being away down there exposed to everything."

By the next April Madison's letters were coming from Tennessee. "Lizzie, I am sorry you are so lonely without me," he wrote. "You seem to wonder that I should wish to be in a battle. I do not wish to be in a battle just for the sake of killing anybody, but we enlisted to conquer the enemies of the Union."

Jane Grey Swisshelm was one Minnesotan who spoke out against slavery. When she came to the state in 1857, she was a well-known writer and editor. She made her home in St. Cloud and started a newspaper there. In the paper she called for an end to slavery.

Many people blamed Jane Swisshelm for the freeing of Eliza Winston, though she had nothing to do with it. One night a crowd of men wrecked her office and dumped her printing press into the river. Her friends helped buy a new press, and she kept the newspaper going. She also made speeches about civil rights for blacks and women. Although women could not vote then, she helped start the Republican party in Minnesota and worked to elect Abraham Lincoln as president. During the Civil War Jane Swisshelm returned to the East and became a nurse with the Union army.

Within a few weeks Madison had his wish. Shocked, he described to Lizzie "the shouts of charging squadrons, plunging horses, falling with dead and living riders, the terrific roar of artillery and volleys of infantry firing, and the horrifying sight of the mangled, ghastly dead and dying. The first wounded man I saw was just after the first charge. I went to see what I could do for him. My heart melted in pity at the sight. He belonged to the 2nd Georgia Cavalry. He begged for water, which I gave him, and then placed his hat over his face to keep the sun from it. I asked him how he felt, to which he calmly replied that he could bear it. The poor fellow died in a few hours."

As the first months of cheering and marching and flag-waving turned into years of blood and sorrow and destruction, the soldiers' letters changed. There was anger that the war might not settle anything. As the armies moved into the South, northern men got a closer look at slavery. What they saw made them decide that it had to end. Finally President Lincoln signed the Emancipation Proclamation, which freed all slaves in the rebel states on January 1, 1863.

Minnesota's New Pilgrims

When news that slavery had ended reached the South, most black people waited to see how the war would go. Others headed north. It was dangerous, but they were determined to be free. Some volunteered to fight for the Union. Madison Bowler was one of the officers chosen to train them as soldiers in the army.

Madison Bowler and Lizzie Caleff were married during the war, when he came home on leave. Their first child was born while Madison was away with the army.

In Missouri a black man named Robert Hickman agreed with other slaves to make their escape. They lived near the Mississippi River, so, working in secret, they built a crude boat. One night they stole away, got on board, and headed upstream. There may have been as many as two hundred of them.

The group called themselves "the pilgrims." There are many stories about how they made the trip. One tells of help they got from Union soldiers. Another tells how they were towed behind a steamboat. At last they reached St. Paul. In Minnesota things had changed in the three years since Eliza Winston had come up the river with her owner. The pilgrims were welcomed. Some went on to Minneapolis and Stillwater, but most of them stayed in St. Paul. Hickman had been a preacher among his fellow slaves. He and his followers joined together in Minnesota's first black congregation, the Pilgrim Baptist Church.

As the war went on, more blacks came to Minnesota. Most of them settled in St. Paul and Minneapolis. Wartime brought high prices for Minnesota wheat and lumber. There was prosperity, and workers were needed. So the new black Minnesotans were able to find jobs. They could not yet vote in their adopted state, but after the war ended Minnesota's constitution was changed. At last black men became full citizens. Black women, like all others, had to wait another 50 years to vote.

Robert Hickman, the leader of "the pilgrims," had learned to read, write, and preach the Bible as a slave.

Civil War soldiers in training at Fort Snelling

Chapter 11
War at Home

Dakota Anger Explodes

The Civil War was not the only barrier between Minnesotans and their dreams of a great future. An even more terrible struggle held back the rush toward growth and progress. This was the last desperate effort of Indian Minnesotans to regain the country they had lost through the treaties of 1851.

The Dakota had signed the treaties of Traverse des Sioux and Mendota in 1851 because they were sure that without the money from the government they would starve. Ten years later, it seemed that they might starve anyway. By 1862 they were crowded onto a strip of land only ten miles wide along the south side of the Minnesota River. The country that had been theirs was filling up with farms and small towns. Some of the Dakota had also built houses and barns and tried to become farmers. But most of them still hunted for what animals they could find and waited for the treaty payments. When the money was late, they went hungry.

In 1862 the United States was in the middle of the Civil War. Government officials were busy with things they thought more important than paying the Indians. Weeks went by and the treaty money did not come. As the Dakota grew hungrier and more angry, some talked of war. Most of the white men were off fighting in the South. Now was the time to take back their land, they thought. Little Crow and other leaders shook their heads and said it was hopeless.

Then one day a gang of young Dakota, daring each other to prove how brave they were, killed a family of white settlers. They were sure they would be punished and they ran to their people, begging for help. Their story was like a match in a can of gasoline. The Dakota knew that Indians who murdered white people were quickly hanged. They also knew that white men who murdered Indians were seldom punished.

An angry crowd of Dakota went to Little Crow and asked him to lead them in war. He answered no. They said they would fight even if he was afraid to join them. "You are fools," Little Crow told them. "You will be hunted like rabbits in winter. But I am not a coward. I will die with you."

Indians attacked the town of New Ulm twice during the Dakota War. This painting shows the second battle.

Death on the Prairie

Alomina Hurd

Not all of the Dakota joined in the war, but all of them suffered for it. Many unsuspecting white people suffered, too. There was burning and killing, and the green grass of the Minnesota Valley was stained with blood. Surprised settlers, who saw a nearby farm in flames or who met their neighbors running in panic, fled to the nearest town or to Fort Ridgely. Some were too late.

Those who lived near Lake Shetek in Murray County had a long way to go—nearly 60 miles to the town of New Ulm. Phineas and Alomina Hurd had farmed there for three years. They knew many of the Indians who came to the lake from time to time. Alomina had even learned to speak a little of the Dakota language.

Phineas was away from home on the morning of August 20, 1862, when a group of Dakota rode up. Alomina recognized one of the horses as her husband's and became alarmed. The hired man ran into the yard and one of the Indians shot and killed him. Then the Dakota rushed into the house and began to destroy everything in it. But they said they would not harm Alomina.

Later she told how "I was ordered to take the children and depart at once. The youngest child I took in my arms, and led the other (a boy, then three years old) by the hand. The Indians accompanied me a short distance from the house. Thus I was left, with my two children almost naked, myself bareheaded, without food or even a blanket. My little boy, William Henry,

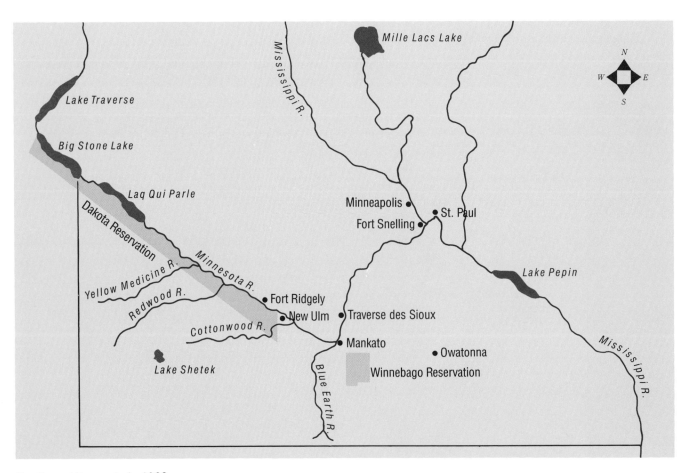

Southern Minnesota in 1862

being barefooted and thinly clad, shivered with the cold, and cried pitifully at first. But after a time, pressing my hand, he trudged manfully along by my side. The little one rested in my arms. Two guns were fired when I was a short distance out, which told the death of my neighbor, Mr. Koch. I well knew its fearful meaning. There was death behind, and all the horrors of starvation before me."

Soon a thunderstorm came up. In the rain Alomina lost her way, and for two days she wandered around on the prairie. Then she found the road leading to New Ulm. At first William Henry cried for food. Later he became sick. By the end of the third day he was too weak to walk. Alomina was nursing the baby, and she was also becoming weak. "I could no longer carry both my children at the same time, but took one a distance of a quarter or half a mile, laid it in the grass, and returned for the other. In this way I traveled twelve miles to a place called Dutch-Charley's."

To her surprise and despair, the house was empty. But in the garden were carrots and onions. She also found a small chunk of spoiled ham. With this food her little boy got better, and they were able to walk another 25 miles. There they met up with other fleeing settlers, some badly hurt. Soon the refugees found a deserted farm, where they stayed until a rescue party came from New Ulm. Only then did Alomina learn that fighting had spread all across western Minnesota, and "the sad, sickening thought was now fully confirmed in my mind that my husband was dead."

These white farmers and missionaries, fleeing from the Dakota, camped together on the prairie.

The Tide Turns

Many settlers fled to Fort Ridgely. It was a small outpost on a bluff above the Minnesota River. It had no walls and only a few soldiers. But the fort did have two cannons and a man who knew how to shoot them well. Twice the Dakota attacked. Both times the soldiers and settlers, helped by the cannons, drove them back. Big Eagle *(Wam-mdi-tan-ka),* one of the Dakota men who fought there, said later, "We thought the fort was the door to the valley. But the defenders of the fort were very brave and kept the door shut."

There was also fighting at New Ulm and in other places. Slowly the tide turned against the Dakota. An army of volunteers led by Henry Sibley marched to Fort Ridgely and then on up the Minnesota Valley. On the way they found the bodies of settlers killed in the first Dakota attacks. They were horrified. Sibley, who had traded with the Dakota for many years, wrote to his wife, "My heart is hardened against them beyond any touch of mercy."

The Dakota who had taken no part in the war were eager for peace. The family of Good Star Woman *(Wi-kan-hpi-wa-śte-win)* was among them. She was eight years old then. Many years later she remembered how she and her mother had been gathering firewood one morning in August. When they heard shooting, they hurried back to their camp. Soon an Indian man rode up, so shocked he could hardly speak. "The Dakota are killing the whites," he finally told them. Some of the Dakota who joined in the war turned against those who did not. Good Star Woman remembered being placed in a trench with other children to be safe from attack by either side.

One Who Appears

Little Crow

118

The followers of Little Crow were defeated in a battle in Yellow Medicine County, and at last the peaceful group could make a truce. They set free more than two hundred white captives whom they had protected from harm.

Little Crow and others who would not give up got on their horses and rode away to the west and north. Some went to Canada, where their descendants still live. Some joined the western bands of the tribe. As Little Crow had said, they were hunted like rabbits. The state of Minnesota paid rewards for Dakota scalps.

Punishing the Dakota

The rest of the Dakota were divided into two groups. Soldiers guarded the men while a court of army officers and government officials tried to judge which ones had taken part in the fighting. They found more than three hundred guilty and said that all of them should be hanged. Most white Minnesotans agreed. Only a few thought it was unjust to hang a man because he had fought for his people. One who felt that way was the Episcopal bishop, Henry B. Whipple. When no one in Minnesota would hear him, he went to Washington and told President Lincoln how the Dakota had been cheated and starved. Lincoln listened. He allowed only 38 of the Dakota to be hanged. The others were sent to prison.

The second group of Dakota were the women, children, grandparents, and a few men who could prove that they had not joined in the war. These people were told they must go to Fort Snelling. Good Star

Little Crow led the Dakota in war against the Americans, though he had told his people not to fight. Among the Dakota a leader's power depended on the respect of his followers. Little Crow was a man who could make himself respected. He was strong and self-confident. He had a sharp memory and a gift for public speaking. He was also ambitious.

Little Crow's father and grandfather had been leaders of the Kaposia band. His grandfather (also called Little Crow) had signed the treaties allowing the United States to build Fort Snelling. Little Crow was certain he would be chief. But he had a habit of getting into trouble. As a young man, he left Kaposia and went westward. Marrying a woman of another Dakota band, he lived among her people. Then his father died in an accident and his brother tried to become chief. Little Crow returned to Kaposia.

In the fight that followed, the brother was killed and Little Crow was wounded. A bullet went through

both his wrists, breaking the bones. His friends took him to the army doctor at Fort Snelling. The doctor shook his head and said Little Crow would die unless both hands were removed. Little Crow replied he would rather die. He returned to Kaposia. There he was treated by a Dakota medicine man. Although he got back the use of his hands, they were crooked for the rest of his life.

Government agents usually wished Little Crow were somewhere else when treaties were discussed. He was tough at bargaining and the Dakota always listened to him. He remembered exactly what promises had been made to his people. Never did he fail to remind the white men when these were not kept. But Little Crow had been to Washington. He knew the power of the Americans. Time after time he warned his people that fighting was useless.

In 1862, after Little Crow agreed to lead the Dakota in war, he said: "I will die with you." His words came true. The Dakota were overcome in battle, and Little Crow went to

Canada. He was ready to stop fighting. But he returned to Minnesota to get some horses. With him went his 16-year-old son, One Who Appears *(Wo-wi-na-pe)*. One afternoon the father and son stopped to pick some wild berries. Two farmers saw them. They were alarmed at the sight of Indians. Without waiting to ask questions, they hid in some bushes and started shooting.

Little Crow was hit, but he fired back. Then another bullet hit him. He fell to the ground. One of the farmers was wounded, too. The other farmer crept away through the tall grass and ran for help. One Who Appears crawled to his father, who asked for water. The boy brought him some and stayed with Little Crow until he died. Then, knowing that more white men would come soon, One Who Appears covered his father's body with a blanket and fled.

White Minnesotans rejoiced when they learned that the Dakota leader they feared most was dead. The state gave a reward of $500 to the farmer who shot him.

Woman's father was one. She remembered: "The soldiers brought wagons for the women and children, while the Indians who had horses took them and put their belongings on travois." Her father had a horse, so she and her two younger sisters rode on the travois. Fearing the whites, her father covered the three little girls with a buffalo hide. It was a good idea.

Soldiers guarded the Dakota during the long, sad trip, but they were not always able to protect them. Good Star Woman remembered peeking from under the buffalo skin as they passed through towns where "the people brought poles, pitchforks, and axes and hit some of the women and children in the wagons." Once her father was struck and almost knocked down. A few Indians were hurt so badly that they died. Their friends buried them at night and tried to hide the graves. They feared that whites would find the bodies and take the scalps for a reward.

At Fort Snelling the Dakota camped on the flat land along the river, where they had often met for games and dances in earlier times. A high fence around their camp did not keep whites from stealing their horses and oxen. All winter they stayed there. So many died from measles and other sickness that they had to be buried in long trenches. Good Star Woman's sister was one. Another was Cloud Man, the first Dakota to try farming.

President Lincoln wrote to Henry Sibley, listing the names of 38 Dakota against whom there was evidence of crime. He warned Sibley to protect the Indians from "unlawful violence."

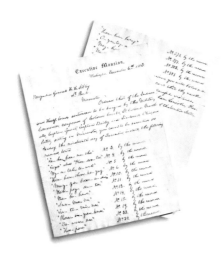

Dakota people traveling with a horse and travois

120

In the spring the Dakota were loaded on steamboats. They were taken down the Mississippi River and up the Missouri to a camp in what is now South Dakota. There they were kept for two years. The government was supposed to send food, but—just like the treaty money—it was never enough and always too late. Some of the women and old men planted corn, but no rain fell and the corn withered. A few hunted, but it was a barren place and there were few animals. Many died from hunger and disease. At last the long nightmare ended. The Dakota were moved to a better place in Nebraska, and the men in prison were set free to join their families.

Afterward

No one knows exactly how many people were killed in Minnesota during the Dakota War. As many as 500 settlers may have died. Not many Dakota were killed at first, but hundreds died later on the plains of North and South Dakota.

The Dakota were not the only Indians who suffered from the fear and hatred that the war aroused among Minnesotans. The Winnebago, a Wisconsin tribe, had a small reservation in the fertile Blue Earth Valley of southern Minnesota. Even though they took no part in the war, they were driven from their farms and sent to the Missouri River with the Dakota.

A soldier who fought at Fort Ridgely during the Dakota attacks later painted this picture.

The Ojibway did not join the war either. But nervous settlers in central Minnesota demanded that Indians at places like Mille Lacs and Gull Lake move away. Beginning in 1863, government officials worked at schemes to put all the Ojibway on one big reservation far to the north. At last, in 1867, they decided on White Earth. The government tried many ways to make the Ojibway go to the White Earth Reservation. Those at Gull Lake moved. Some Indian families were moved from Mille Lacs and their houses were burned. In the end many returned anyway.

For white Minnesotans, their young state's experience of blood and terror wiped away all promises to the Dakota. Also gone were feelings of guilt about how the Indians were treated. Stories and history books told about the great "Minnesota Massacre" and described the Dakota as terrible savages. None gave the Indian side. Stone monuments in the Minnesota Valley still mark places where battles were fought and where white people were killed.

Settlement in western Minnesota stopped for a time. But with the Civil War over and the Indians pushed out of the way, thousands of people again turned westward. In a few years all the rich prairie that had belonged to the Dakota was turned into farms.

The Dakota prison camp below Fort Snelling

Christian Dakota in the camp at Fort Snelling gathered at a service led by Bishop Henry Whipple.

"Straight Tongue" was what Indian friends called Henry Benjamin Whipple. An Episcopal minister, Whipple was named bishop of Minnesota in 1859. Almost at once, he visited the state's Indian communities and supported mission work there. The cheating he saw by government agents who were supposed to be helping Indians angered him.

In 1862 Whipple spoke out against taking revenge on all Dakota for the war started by a few. He reminded Minnesotans that many Dakota had not joined Little Crow. He showed that the peaceful Dakota had saved hundreds of white captives. But no one would listen.

After the war, Whipple kept working to get more just treatment for Indians. But like other white men of his time, he wanted them to give up their language, their customs, their tribal ties, and their religion.

Unit IV
New People and New Patterns on the Land

Chapter 12
Breaking the Sod

Getting Started

The settlers who turned Minnesota's prairies and woodlands into farms talked about breaking "new" land. They paid in sweat, calluses, and aching backs to cut through the heavy tangle of roots called sod. For thousands of years the roots in the sod had fed plants that gave food and shelter to insects, birds, and animals. Those, in turn, had made life possible for people. The thick sod also protected the soil beneath it and stored water during dry seasons. But few settlers thought much about the ancient natural system they ripped apart.

Like everyone else, settlers were in a hurry. Many did not wait for surveyors to measure and mark the land. They moved in before the government was ready to sell. Then Congress decided to give farms away and passed the Homestead Act. Those who voted for it thought that giving land to farmers would get the country settled even faster. The sooner it was settled, they said, the larger, richer, and more powerful the nation would be.

They also argued that free land would let anyone, no matter how poor, become a farmer. But a farm was more than land. It was also a house, a barn, fences, tools, animals, seed, and many more things. All of them took money. Even with free land, a farmer often had to borrow money to get started.

A settler in Minnesota had to own a plow and a harrow, an ax, a spade, a pitchfork, and a scythe or a grain cradle. Without these tools farmers could not start work. A wagon and a team of oxen to pull it were also needed. Few early farmers could afford horses. Oxen were slow-moving but strong. They were good for pulling heavy loads and for plowing. And they were hardy and easy to feed. Many families also had a cow or two and a few chickens or pigs.

After farmers had decided on their claims or homesteads, the next things they needed were shelter and water. If there were woods, logs could be cut for a cabin. On the treeless prairies of southern and western Minnesota, houses and barns were often made from blocks of sod. When

Thomas P. Rossiter painted this view of a Minnesota prairie farm in 1865. The cone-shaped stacks might be either straw left after threshing wheat or hay cut to feed cattle. The cranelike structure beside the house holds a bucket on a rope for drawing water from a well.

A Family Affair

Above is a cradle, used for cutting grain by hand. Below, farmers help each other break sod.

these were piled in layers, the tough roots kept out rain and snow. If the building was on a hillside, only the roof and one wall were made from sod. Such a house was called a dugout. In Minnesota, heat for sod houses and log cabins was likely to come from an iron stove instead of a fireplace. For light, settlers used some candles, but mostly kerosene lamps.

Unless there was a lake or stream nearby, the farmer had to dig a well. In most parts of Minnesota that was not hard because the water table was high. This means that underground water was very near the surface. Pure water could usually be pulled up in buckets.

When the first settlers came to Minnesota, wire fences were not yet being made. Wood for rail fences was costly unless it could be cut from nearby trees. Building fences was slow work. So in the early years most farmers fenced their fields of grain and the vegetable gardens but not their animals. Cows and pigs could roam on open land and find food. Children often had to watch the animals and keep them from wandering too far.

Every member of the farm family had jobs to do. In the 1800s there was a strict line between what was thought to be "man's work" and "woman's work." Both were important to keeping the farm going. Of course, when there was a real need, people got the job done no matter whose work it was supposed to be.

For men, pioneer farming meant heavy work in the fields. When a farmer was not busy plowing, planting, or harvesting crops, he had to repair buildings or tools. Animals had to be cared for every day. If the farm

was new, he spent some time each year plowing more land and adding to the buildings and fences. It was hard to start a farm alone. A man needed a wife to help him. Women seldom tried farming alone, although a woman with teenage children or money for hired men sometimes ran a farm.

There is an old saying: "Man's work lasts from sun to sun, but woman's work is never done." A farm woman's jobs ended only when her strength ran out. Cooking, cleaning, washing, and caring for young children were just the beginning. She also made soap and sometimes candles, sewed and mended clothes, and put up fruits and vegetables for winter. If there were cows, she made butter or cheese. If there were chickens, she had to care for them. The vegetable garden was usually her job, too.

As soon as children were big enough, they carried firewood and brought water from the well. Weeding the garden, gathering eggs, and bringing in the cows for milking were other chores for boys and girls. When they were older they helped in the fields or cared for younger brothers and sisters.

Summer was the busiest time on farms. For that reason country schools always closed between spring and fall. Farm children often dropped out of school after a few years. That did not mean they were uneducated. Working beside their parents, they learned many skills that people today have forgotten.

There were good things about farm life. Working together led people to understand each other. All members of the family, even the oldest grandparents, knew they were needed. Being a neighbor was important, too.

A Norwegian settler and her sod house near Madison, in Lac qui Parle County. Such houses often had wooden doors and window frames with glass to let in light.

Farm families often shared heavy jobs like building a barn or harvesting a crop. When the work was done, people had fun celebrating together. In times of sickness or trouble, neighbors helped each other.

But there could be loneliness, too. In the early years farms were far apart and roads were bad. A trip to the nearest town often took many hours. If so, the husband usually went alone. Weeks might pass without his wife having a chance to see or talk to anyone but her family.

Good Times and Bad

Early farmers generally looked forward to better times. They felt sure they were building for the future. The farm would pass on to their children and grandchildren. Their own hard work would mean an easier life for those to come.

This was easy to believe in the first ten years after Minnesota became a state. The Civil War was going on. Armies had to be fed. The price of grain was high, and the new soil was wonderfully rich. These boom times made river towns like Red Wing, Winona, and Hastings into busy wheat markets.

Farmers in southeastern Minnesota hurried to plow more ground. Many of them also bought new machines to speed up their work. Only a few years earlier, an inventor named Cyrus McCormick had built a reaper that could cut grain faster than a dozen men working by hand. Soon there were machines for doing other fieldwork too.

German farmers in Stearns County pitch hay by hand in the 1870s.

Minnesota was a good place to use these machines. The ground was level. There were few big stones. Land was easy to get, so fields could be large. During the 1860s farmers in the settled parts of the state bought hundreds of reapers, mowers, rakes, seed drills, and threshing machines. They also had to buy horses to pull them. Oxen were too slow and clumsy.

Then times turned bad. In the 1870s crop prices fell. This was hardest on new farmers just getting started in the western counties of Minnesota. Soon a worse disaster struck. High in the air they saw strange, silvery clouds. As these came closer, people found that the clouds were millions of grasshoppers. When the insects came to the ground, they ate everything in sight. Farmers watched in horror as the hungry 'hoppers mowed down their fields of wheat. Farm families lost a whole year's work in a day or two.

For five years, from 1873 through 1877, farms in the western part of the state were left bare by grasshoppers. There was no welfare system or government aid for farmers. Friends and neighbors tried to help, but everyone was poor. So was the county government. People sent letters to the governor, begging for help.

One discouraged Brown County woman told of how her husband borrowed money for new seed after grasshoppers ate their crops. Then the same thing happened the next year. This time they sold their horses to buy seed. Again the grasshoppers came. Now they had nothing left to sell and nothing for the family to eat. Another woman wrote from near Alexandria:

A horse-drawn hay rake

Farmers in the 1870s had no sprays to kill insects. They tried many ways to fight grasshoppers, but none worked. Here they are shown scooping them up in nets.

"We have not bought any clothing since we came here, for it has took all we could raise to live, without buying clothes. My husband has not had a sock on his feet this winter, and he suffers very much with the cold."

The governor called on people in towns and cities to help. Churches collected food and clothes for people in the western counties. The state government sent food, too, and bought new seed for many farmers. At last the grasshoppers left, as suddenly as they had come.

Farmers Get Together

Other problems did not go away. Farmers found that they could not prosper just by raising good crops. They had to be able to sell them. When farms were smaller and all work was done by hand, most of what a farm produced was used by the family itself. The little left over was traded or sold in the nearest town. This is called subsistence farming.

Minnesotans who grew large crops of grain for sale in distant places were market farmers. Unless they could sell their crops, they had no way to pay for buildings, fences, machines, and horses. A wagonload of wheat had to be hauled to a place where it could be put on a steamboat or train and shipped to market. Farmers hoped for more railroads, but when they got them, the problems did not end. In hard times farmers were paid less for their wheat. But railroad rates stayed the same. So did the cost of machinery. So did interest payments on borrowed money. It seemed that the harder farmers worked, the poorer they got. Soon they became angry. They felt cheated.

Ignatius Donnelly was not a full-time farmer, but he raised some wheat on land he owned. For 30 years he also raised trouble for Minnesota politicians.

During the 1860s Donnelly served in Congress. Later he started several newspapers and wrote half a dozen books that were read all over the world. But in his own state he was best known for leadership of farmers and workers in their demand for more power.

Donnelly was one of Minnesota's favorite speakers. There was neither radio nor television then, but he traveled by stagecoach and train all over the state. People came for miles to hear his stories, chuckle at his jokes, and listen to his arguments. His razor-sharp wit made his enemies wince. One story tells how someone in the audience threw a rotten cabbage at him. He picked it up and said: "I asked you to give me your ears, not your head."

Plowing with horses in the 1880s

Plenty of people were ready to tell them what to do about it. Some argued that farmers should get together and vote. Get laws passed, they said, to make railroad companies and banks treat farmers fairly. Over the years farmers formed several political groups in Minnesota. One was the Anti-Monopoly party. Others were the Farmers Alliance and the People's party, sometimes called the Populists.

Others saw the answer in organizations that would make farmers proud of themselves and lead them to help each other. One such group was the Patrons of Husbandry. Its local branches were called granges. Members were told they were "the strength of the nation" and that farming was "the highest calling on earth." Grange members sometimes formed buying clubs to get machinery at lower prices or to cooperate in other ways.

Another idea was to learn better farming methods. Teachers, scientists, and even many farm leaders argued that farms would produce more if farmers knew more about soil and plants and breeding animals. They should get away from raising just one kind of crop. Scientific farming was better business. The granges and other groups urged the state's colleges to teach these things to farmers.

The Changed Land

Minnesota farmers listened to all of this advice. They kept on protesting against the power of railroads and big companies. They formed business organizations called cooperatives to get better prices on what they bought and sold. And they looked for different kinds of crops and more animals to raise.

Eva McDonald was a young working woman from Minneapolis with a talent for politics. In 1889 she spoke for the Farmers Alliance in small towns across Minnesota. "Why," she asked, "are farmers the hardest working and poorest paid class in the country while railroad companies, real estate speculators, and stock gamblers grow wealthy without doing any work at all?"

Minnesota women could not vote or join the Farmers Alliance. Eva McDonald thought they should be members and said so. Her blunt words and spitfire temper made enemies for her in Minnesota. Later, speaking for the People's party, she talked in other states about the problems of farm families. She said she would go on "as long as there are homeless, voiceless women, helpless to cope with the hard conditions of life."

Producing a variety of things is called diversified farming. It takes more work and know-how than growing just one kind of crop. It also takes more money for buildings and machinery. But slowly, between 1870 and 1900, most Minnesota farms became diversified. There were other changes, too. People moved from sod houses and log cabins into farmhouses of neatly sawed boards. At first these looked ugly and bare, alone on the prairie. Then farmers planted trees for shelter from sun and wind and for firewood. Here and there some even found time to plant a climbing rosebush or a hedge of lilacs.

When land grew harder to get, ditches were dug to drain away water from swamps and shallow lakes. These became fields and pastures. As the water ran off down streams and rivers, the level of underground water also fell. Wells had to be deeper and pumps were needed. So farmers put up windmills to pump water. With more cows, horses, pigs, and even some sheep, barns had to be bigger. Wire fences kept the animals from roaming. Corn and alfalfa for feed were stored in corncribs and silos.

Children who had crawled or toddled across the floors of sod houses were now grown men and women with children of their own. By the 1890s the whole landscape of southern and western Minnesota had changed. In the east, woodlands had become fields. In the west, the wide sea of waving grass or grain no longer stretched from skyline to skyline. It was boxed in by groves of trees and clumps of buildings.

Everywhere the straight lines of fences and roads cut across the curves of river valleys and hillsides. The lines followed surveyors' bound-

Oliver H. Kelley, an early Minnesota farmer, dreamed of organizing a "brotherhood" of farmers. In 1867 he and a few friends founded the Patrons of Husbandry. Most people liked a shorter name and called it the Grange. It spread across the country like wildfire.

Kelley himself believed in "scientific" farming. He thought the mission of the Grange should be education. Others disagreed. Many members turned to politics. The laws they got passed to regulate railroads are sometimes called Granger laws.

From his farm south of Elk River, Kelley promoted the Grange for several years. Then he moved to Washington, D.C., and later to Florida. He was a hearty, enthusiastic man. Once he claimed to be "as full of public spirit as a dog is full of fleas."

Caroline Hall, a young Wright County teacher, was the niece of Oliver H. Kelley. She shared his dream of farmers supporting and encouraging each other. They often discussed it in letters. Then she helped Kelley promote the Grange and worked in its office for many years.

Because of Caroline Hall, the Grange was the first large farm organization with women and men as equal members. She insisted that it be a sisterhood as well as a brotherhood. Whole families joined the Grange and took part in activities like picnics and lectures. This proved to be one of its greatest strengths.

A "brush breaker" plow, 1870s

132

ary marks. These had carved up the land into square sections like a checkerboard so it could be measured and sold. County courthouses were filled with maps and records that told who owned each square.

At least a part of the pioneer farmers' dreams had come true. The rich land that had belonged to the Dakota Indians was home for thousands of white people. On it they grew food that supplied cities all over the world. But the change had cost something. Part of the cost was in the suffering of the Dakota people. Another part was paid by the men and women who spent their lives turning the land into farms.

An author named Hamlin Garland wrote about growing up on a new farm near the border of Minnesota and Iowa. He remembered it as a grim round of work, winter and summer. There were few holidays and no vacations. Building up the country had meant no rug for the floor and no paint on the house. Always more land or a piece of machinery came first. Books were few, and chances to read them were fewer. Even a chance to talk with new people seldom came along. Minds were starved and backs became bent. Garland's deepest sorrow was at the sight of his mother. Never-ending drudgery had made her gray and sad-eyed long before she was old.

But by the end of the 1800s it seemed that the hardest struggle was past. Looking at miles of fields and homesteads, farm families could feel a weary pride. As they saw it, they had tamed a wild, new country and made it produce more than anyone had dreamed. They had come to love it almost as the Dakota had. Now, they thought, their children only needed to live on it and care for it.

This typical Minnesota farm of the 1890s had cattle and horses, barbed wire fences, a large barn and farmhouse, and a windmill to pump water for both animals and people.

Oren C. Gregg spent most of his life teaching other farmers how to improve their farms. He grew up in Vermont. First he wanted to be a minister. Then he decided on farming. After the Civil War he moved to southwestern Minnesota.

There he and his wife Charlotte created a model dairy farm. They were the first Minnesota farmers to get cows to produce milk through the harsh winter months. Charlotte Gregg's "Solid Gold" butter won prizes at the state fair.

In the 1880s farmers complained that courses in agriculture at the University of Minnesota did nothing for them. Gregg suggested to university officials that they hold meetings (called institutes) for farmers all over the state. He also suggested hiring teachers who had farmed themselves. So they asked him to run such a program.

Gregg's institutes were so successful they continued for nearly 20 years. In 1894 the Gregg farm in Lyon County became the university's first agricultural experiment station.

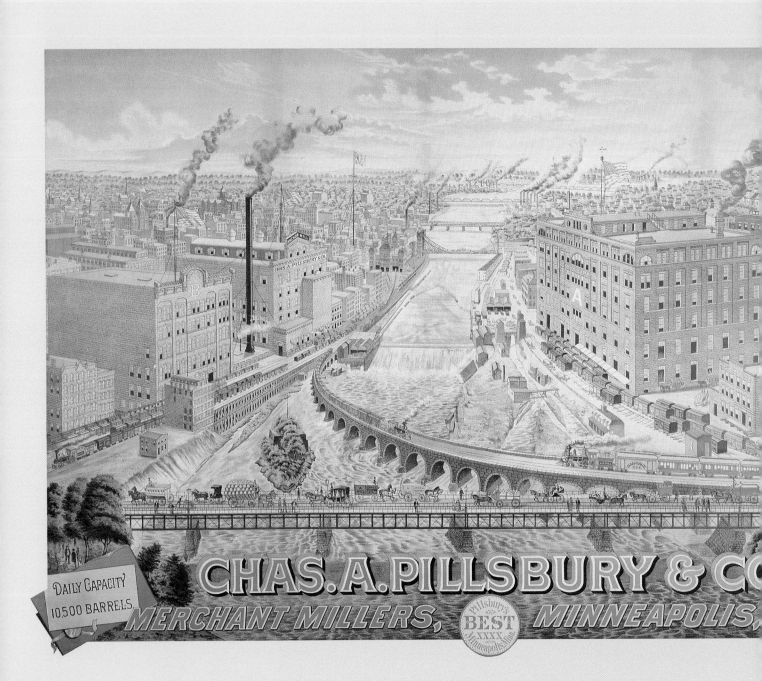

Chapter 13
Towns, Timber, and Iron Rails

The Railroad Age

While farmers turned prairies and woodlands into fields and pastures, other changes were going on, too. The lumber industry that had started in the St. Croix Valley spread across the northeastern part of the state. More and bigger sawmills turned trees into boards. Huge flour mills with new and better machines replaced the small mills that had served early settlers. Villages and towns, then cities, grew up. New businesses and industries were added. All of these changes depended on railroads.

The pattern of towns and transportation seen in the state today was set during the age of railroad building. In Minnesota this lasted from the end of the Civil War to the early 1900s. By 1868 you could travel from the East Coast to St. Paul or Minneapolis by train. Over the next 30 years, two railroad lines linked Minnesota with the West Coast. At the time this dream of the early settlers came true, you could also take a train to almost any town in the state. Meanwhile government land grants had given about one-fifth of Minnesota's area to railroad companies.

All across western Minnesota, towns like Hawley, started by railroads, had grown into busy communities. Others, planned in the same way, never made it. Some villages faded away when the iron rails bypassed them. The settlement at Crow Wing was an example. In the 1860s it was a busy trading center on the Mississippi at the mouth of the Crow Wing River. It had houses, hotels, and stores. White settlers and Indian people came there to buy and sell goods. Long lines of Red River carts passed through each summer. A stagecoach carried passengers and mail to and from St. Paul. Then in 1870 the Northern Pacific Railroad built its track across the Mississippi about ten miles above Crow Wing. There the company founded Brainerd. Buildings and businesses were moved to the new place. Within a few years Crow Wing was a ghost town.

This drawing, from an advertisement for the Pillsbury flour milling company of Minneapolis, shows how the city had grown by the mid-1880s. Two trains meet on the graceful Stone Arch Bridge over the Mississippi River. Railroad builder James J. Hill planned the bridge to be "the finest structure of the kind on the Continent."

Jay Cooke's City

Railroads decided the fate of cities too. Duluth might have been a sleepy fishing village or a suburb of Superior, Wisconsin, without the Northern Pacific. The change began in the summer of 1868, when interest in railroads brought west a party of wealthy businessmen and bankers from the city of Philadelphia. The leader of the group was Jay Cooke.

They traveled aboard a Great Lakes steamship and landed at the town of Superior. Still dressed in the clothes of eastern gentlemen, complete with top hats and walking sticks, they hired some Indian people with a big canoe to take them across the bay. From the water Cooke saw Duluth—about two dozen rough buildings strung along the Minnesota shore. But he was really looking at the deep, quiet harbor. How easy it would be, he may have thought, to dig a canal through the sandbar that divided the bay from the open lake. On the hills above he could see the beginning of rich pine forests that stretched for miles. He had heard that some people thought the hills held iron ore, too.

In his mind Cooke pictured a line of rails going straight west through Minnesota and across the plains and mountains to the Pacific. He could see trains loaded with all the lumber, wheat, cattle, and other products of the northwestern region steaming into Duluth. There ships would take the freight, then carry it across the Great Lakes to cities in the East. The vision looked good.

The harbor towns of Duluth and Superior about 1870. The railroad track into Duluth was shared by the Northern Pacific and the line that ran to St. Paul. Both were controlled by Jay Cooke.

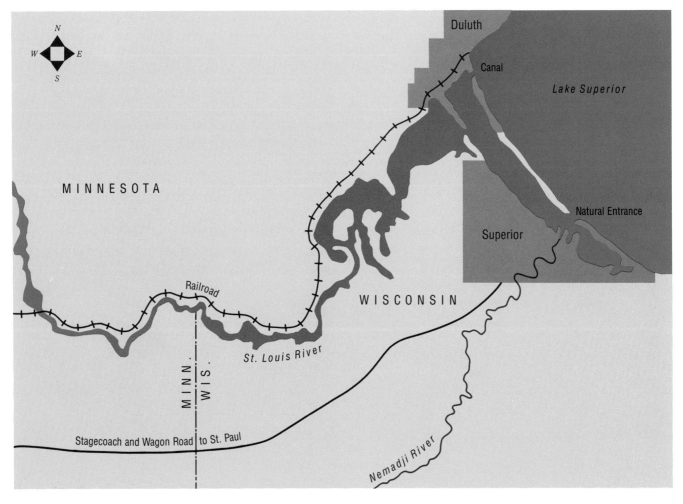

Back in Philadelphia, Cooke bought the stock of a railroad that Minnesota businessmen were building from St. Paul to Duluth. Then he put together plans to raise money for the Northern Pacific. He did not forget to buy up a lot of the land in and around Duluth.

By the next spring the village was a boom town. People said it would soon be another Chicago. The editor of its new newspaper had a talent for high-flown words. He called Duluth "the Zenith City of the unsalted seas." Houses could not be built fast enough for all the railroad workers, land buyers, and other newcomers.

By the end of 1870 track had been laid between Duluth and St. Paul. According to one traveler, "The railroad right of way was cleared 50 feet wide. It was a straight hole through the woods, which seemed too narrow for a train to come through in the distance." The trip now took a single day instead of a bone-crunching week by stagecoach. At the same time the track of the Northern Pacific was stretching westward from Duluth. In 1871 it reached the Red River.

Meanwhile, the citizens of Duluth had formed a company to improve the harbor by making a canal through Minnesota Point. First they asked for help from the government. Congress refused. So they started to dig the canal themselves. People in Superior worried that a new opening would change the flow of water in the bay. It might leave the entrance to their own port too shallow for ships. They threatened to take their case to court.

Wooden shacks crowded along the lakeshore at Duluth in 1870.

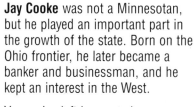

Jay Cooke was not a Minnesotan, but he played an important part in the growth of the state. Born on the Ohio frontier, he later became a banker and businessman, and he kept an interest in the West.

Young Jay left home early, determined to make a name in business. During the Civil War he helped the government sell bonds. With the war over, the United States was in a fever of building and growing. The dream of iron rails crossing the continent and binding the country together from East to West took hold of many business leaders. Cooke thought it could be done. He was right, but he did not count on how much time and money it would take. Raising money to build the Northern Pacific was too big a job for the bank of Jay Cooke & Company. Cooke's firm had to close, and his dream died in the middle of North Dakota.

No one was certain what would happen to the currents in the bay, but Duluth people rushed to dig the canal before a court order could stop them. In late April 1871, they used a dredge to start a ditch 30 feet wide and 8 feet deep across the point. Only a few feet from the lake, a thick layer of frozen gravel stopped the dredge. According to the Duluth newspaper, "Some of our citizens at once turned in with shovels and picks and drills and gunpowder (two kegs), and at one o'clock P.M. the union of the waters became an accomplished fact!" There was a lot of argument afterward in the courts, but the canal was already built. Fortunately it did little harm to the bay.

Two years later came the depression of the 1870s. Banks failed all across the country. The Northern Pacific went broke, and Duluth's boom ended as quickly as it had started. In 1873 the city had about 5,000 people. A year later nearly 4,000 had left. Buildings and land that had been worth thousands of dollars could not be sold at all. A few fishermen and loggers stayed on with their families, and in time Duluth grew again. Meanwhile the railroad map of Minnesota was changing.

Jim Hill Fights Back

Jay Cooke was not the only one with a vision of railroad tracks across the plains and mountains. From the Twin Cities the owners of the St. Paul and Pacific Railroad had started to build a line westward. In 1871 it reached the Red River at Breckenridge, and a branch line was built through St. Cloud. But like the Northern Pacific, the company failed.

Minnesota Point from the hill above Duluth in 1875

With two railroads unable to pay their debts, building of new tracks stopped for a while in Minnesota. Paying for a railroad took a lot of money, and no one in the state had it. But one Minnesotan had a plan and plenty of nerve. He was James J. Hill.

For years after coming from Canada as a young man, Hill stayed in the business of handling freight by boat, stagecoach, and wagon. In 1871 he started a line of steamboats on the Red River. Because there were no railroads across Canada, traffic from Manitoba traveled by river to Moorhead. There it was transferred to the trains of the Northern Pacific.

Hill knew the country, and he had studied the railroads carefully. He could see that the land around Winnipeg was filling with settlers faster than the plains of North Dakota and Montana. He knew the St. Paul and Pacific had started a branch line through the Red River Valley to the Canadian border. And he knew the tracks had to be finished soon or the company would lose its land grant.

Hill had powerful business friends in Canada. They wanted a railroad between Winnipeg and the Twin Cities. With Hill they agreed to buy the St. Paul and Pacific. They would supply the money. Hill was to run the company and get the tracks laid.

After many months of talking and bargaining, they struck a deal. There was barely time left to save the grant. With the will and energy that made him famous, Hill pushed the line ahead. It got done with only days to spare. He and his partners renamed the railroad the St. Paul, Minneapolis, and Manitoba.

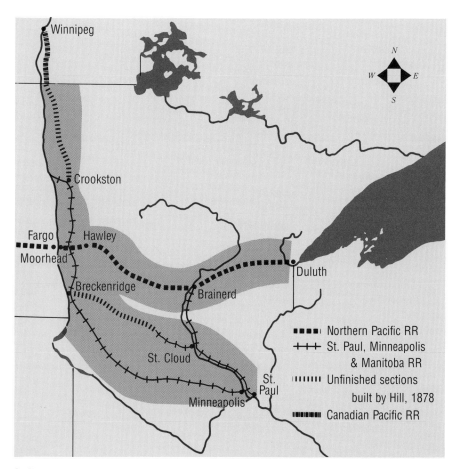

Railroads and land grants in northern and western Minnesota, 1879. In the grant areas (shaded), the railroads owned about half the land.

Map legend:
■■■■ Northern Pacific RR
+++ St. Paul, Minneapolis & Manitoba RR
||||||| Unfinished sections built by Hill, 1878
▥▥▥ Canadian Pacific RR

James J. Hill was often called the Empire Builder. The nickname fit. By the end of his life he was one of the country's most powerful business leaders. For many years he had been the most powerful man in Minnesota. Besides railroads, he owned Great Lakes steamships, coal mines, iron mines, and waterpower. In business he was known for fierce, sometimes unfair competition.

Minnesotans boasted about him and admired him. Many also feared and hated him. People said he controlled both the Democratic and Republican parties in the state. Once a St. Paul newspaper supported a Populist-Democrat for president. Hill did not like it. So he bought the paper and changed the policy.

Hill liked things that lasted. The bridges, tunnels, and buildings that he put up were fine and solid. He was a short, broad-shouldered man with an immense drive to get things done. As a boy of nine, he had an accident with a bow and arrow that left him nearly blind in one eye. Few people ever knew about it.

139

CAN HE STOP THEM?

Minnesota's governor, Samuel R. Van Sant, tried to stop Hill's scheme to merge competing lines.

At Moorhead in the 1870s, the Northern Pacific tracks crossed the Red River on this bridge.

Early in 1879 trains began running over the Manitoba line from Winnipeg to St. Paul. No longer were steamboats needed on the Red River. And no longer did the Northern Pacific get most of the freight. Grain from the Red River Valley and western Canada poured into the Twin Cities instead of Duluth. Some of it was sent on to other places. But most of it went to flour mills in Minneapolis. New owners bought the Northern Pacific and finished its line in 1883. But by then the traffic flow had changed. Northern Pacific trains from the West ran to the Twin Cities, not Lake Superior.

Hill was not yet ready to rest. He, too, dreamed of rails across the continent. During the 1880s he improved the St. Paul, Minneapolis, and Manitoba. Curves and hills along the line were smoothed out so trains could run faster with less cost. He built more tracks, reaching west through North Dakota and Montana. Then with more help from his Canadian friends, Hill reorganized the company under the name Great Northern Railway. In the spring of 1890 he started putting tracks through the mountains to Seattle.

After the Great Northern Railway reached the Pacific Coast, Hill tried to combine it with the Northern Pacific and other lines. By doing so he could control all the main railroads in the northwestern part of the country. But in 1904 the U.S. Supreme Court ruled that this was illegal. There were laws against such monopolies. Highways, trucks, and airlines did not yet exist. All business and travel still depended on railroads. The people of Minnesota seemed to agree with the court that no one should have that much power over their lives.

Lumber Moves from Rivers to Rails

When lumbering started in Minnesota during the 1840s, rivers were still the routes by which everything traveled. Lumberjacks cut timber during the winter. They used oxen or horses to skid the fallen trees over ice to the banks of streams. There they piled them up, waiting for the spring log drive. When the ice was gone and the streams were high, they pushed the logs into the water. Each one was stamped with the log mark of the company.

Skilled "jacks" followed the logs as they floated downstream. They kept them moving and tried to prevent log jams. During a drive thousands of logs poured into the same river from different streams. Before the logs reached the mill, they stopped at a log boom. This was a barrier stretched across the river (sometimes a string of logs chained together). There they were sorted out by the marks of their owners.

The system worked well. But after a few years most of the trees close to streams were gone. To get at the rest, lumbermen had to haul them on rails. Often they built their own tracks. After 1890, when Minnesota lumbering was at its peak, many miles of logging railroads threaded through the northern forests. Lines were laid and timber was cut. Then the rails were taken up for use elsewhere.

In the rush to get timber, companies were not always careful how they did it. The Homestead Act, passed to help small farmers, made it possible for lumbermen to cut trees without paying for them. A company could hire someone to claim a homestead. Loggers cleared the timber,

Logs were marked with brands like these of William D. Washburn and Thomas B. Walker. Below, a log jam on the St. Croix River at Taylors Falls in 1886.

then the "homesteader" left. Thousands of acres in northern Minnesota were logged this way. Companies also bought the right to cut timber without buying the land. This was called stumpage. Lumber companies bought stumpage rights on state land and on Indian reservations. Through cheating and fraud they often paid very little, and the scandal stained Minnesota for many years.

Some lumbermen, however, paid for the land they logged. In 1890 Frederick Weyerhaeuser bought all that was left of the Northern Pacific's land grant in Minnesota. By then the railroad had already sold the good farm land. What Weyerhaeuser got (and wanted) was mostly forest.

However loggers got timber, they left behind a wasteland. Called the cutover, it was miles of tree stumps, chopped branches, bark, and dead brush. In dry years this became a terrible fire hazard. Forest fires were not new to Minnesota. But fires in the northern part of the state at the end of the logging era were worse than anyone could remember. Whole towns were destroyed and hundreds of people died.

Like farming, the lumber industry changed the face of Minnesota. Like railroads, it gave many people jobs and made a few millionaires. And like most Minnesotans of the 1800s, lumbermen saw trees as a resource that only wasted land unless they were cut and used. They felt that by clearing away the forests they were bringing civilization and progress to the state.

Frederick Weyerhaeuser (Wirehowzer) came west as a young immigrant in 1856. He was a soft-spoken man with a German accent and twinkling blue eyes. He did not seem the kind of person likely to lead in the rough-and-tumble lumber industry.

Weyerhaeuser had grown up on a small farm in Germany. When he was 17, his family moved to America. Later he found work at a sawmill on the Mississippi in Rock Island, Illinois. In a few years he became the owner.

When Weyerhaeuser saw that mills farther up the river were getting most of the logs, he began to buy pineland and cut timber himself. Soon the quiet German became known for working with his rivals instead of beating them down. His company grew, and before long he was the most important man in the lumber industry of the Upper Midwest. From western Wisconsin he pushed on to the forests of northern Minnesota. In 1891 he moved his home and main office to St. Paul.

Oxen like these pulled logs in the early days of Minnesota's lumber industry.

After 1890 most logs moved by train, and forests fast disappeared.

The great Hinckley fire was not the biggest forest fire Minnesota ever had. Nor did it take the most lives. But it became the best known.

In 1894 Hinckley was a lumber and railroad town of about 1,200 people. The summer was hot and dry, and fires were a problem. A haze of smoke filled the sky day after day.

On September 1 the citizens had no special reason for fear. The sawmill was running as usual, and trains on the two lines that passed through town were on time. But early in the afternoon a wind rose, smoke grew thicker, and the fire alarm blew. Worried people began to gather at the railroad station. Soon the sky was dark as night. The wind began to roar. It seemed as if a storm were coming. It was—but not rain or hail. It was a firestorm. Within minutes a wall of flame exploded over the town.

Some people climbed into wells. Others reached a nearby pond or the Grindstone River. Two crowded trains got away over burning tracks and bridges. But when daylight came next morning to the smoking ruins of Hinckley, 250 were dead. They were not the only ones. Sandstone and three other villages also burned. No one knows how many people died in the woods between. The fire covered 480 square miles.

These scenes show Hinckley after the fire. Steel tracks near where the depot had stood were twisted by the heat.

Chapter 14
Life in the New State

Forty Years of Statehood

The state of Minnesota was 40 years old in 1898. Most of its million and a half people made their living on farms or in small towns. St. Paul, Minneapolis, and Duluth had begun to grow and change, but they were still medium-sized cities in the middle of broad farm and timber country. Minnesota industries—things like lumber, mining, and flour milling, meat-packing, brewing, and cheese-making—depended on the products of the fields and forests.

Thousands of immigrants had moved to Minnesota from the countries of northern Europe. By 1880 three of every four white Minnesotans were from Europe or had parents who were. In the 1890s they were still coming. Whether at a country crossroad or in a city neighborhood, the first thing a traveler usually noticed was the nationality of the people. Were they Irish? German? Swedish? Czech? Finnish? Russian?

Native-born white Americans still ran the state's government and held nearly all public offices. They were also most of the lawyers, doctors, teachers, and businessmen. But things had begun to change. In 1892 the people of Minnesota for the first time chose a foreign-born governor. He was Knute Nelson, a native of Norway. To the state's many immigrants his election was an important step.

Voting was still a long way off for Minnesota Indian people in the 1890s. Mostly Ojibway, they lived on reservations. They could not travel, buy and sell land, open a business, teach their children, or practice their religion without permission from the U.S. government. Without asking them, Congress voted in 1887 to give each Indian family a farm and sell the rest of their reservation land to white people.

No matter where they came from, most Minnesotans seemed to agree on the importance of schools, churches, and laws. Whether they were immigrants or native-born, they had no patience with the ways of the "Wild West." A visitor to Minneapolis in 1880 wrote: "There is a Yankee flavor of thrift and soberness strangely in contrast with the rough, reckless tone found in the ordinary western burgh."

The same was true in smaller towns. In 1876 the famous outlaw gang led by Jesse James met its end in trying to rob a bank in Northfield. The cashier refused to open the safe (and paid with his life). The townspeople went after the outlaws like a swarm of angry bees. Within a few days most of Jesse's men were dead or in jail.

Herbjorn Gausta painted this scene of Norwegian immigrants gathered at a prayer meeting in the 1880s.

Making a Living

Knute Nelson ran for Congress in 1882 against Charles Kindred, an officer of the Northern Pacific Railroad. Kindred scoffed at him as "a little Norwegian." The description fit. Nelson was short and square, with dark hair, flaming blue eyes, and a temper to match. Voters saw the election as a contest between the railroad and the people. In a campaign marked by threats, fistfights, and riots, they elected the little Norwegian.

Nelson had come from Norway with his mother when he was six. They were very poor. He grew up in Wisconsin, determined to get an education. His schooling was interrupted when he enlisted in the Union army. During the Civil War he was wounded, and he carried a southern bullet in his leg for the rest of his life. After the war he decided to study law.

In 1871 Nelson moved to Alexandria. After serving in the Minnesota legislature and in Congress, he was twice elected governor of the state. Then he became a U.S. senator.

A few people in Minnesota were making the fortunes they had hoped for. Most of them just made a living. There were many ways to do it, and you could nearly always find work at some kind of job.

The timber industry hired hundreds of workers each winter. Lumberjacks earned $1.50 a day. They got meals and a place to sleep, but it was a hard, lonely life. Most of the men were unmarried. Often they worked as field hands on farms during the summer. Others were farmers who left their families and went to the woods to make money cutting timber in the winter, when there was not much farm work needed.

In the 1850s and 1860s logging camps had only one large, low building. The crew cooked meals over a fireplace and slept on the ground. They ate salt pork, beans, and bread three times a day. By the 1880s camps were larger and conditions were better. Bunkhouses had wooden beds with straw mattresses. Stoves were used for heat and cooking. Camp cooks fixed huge meals and served them on long tables. But men still worked from dawn to dark in bitter cold. And tragic accidents could happen when an ax slipped, a tall tree crashed to the ground, or a heavy log rolled without warning.

Albert Onion had a different kind of job in mind. When he came from Vermont in 1878, he was sure "Minneapolis is agoing to be the coming city of the North West." First he worked as a clerk in a grocery. Then he tried several other things. He complained about the high rent and the number of men looking for good places in business.

Lumberjacks sharpen their tools in the bunkhouse of a logging camp.

At last Onion found the right job. He became a salesman, or drummer, as it was called then. Crackers and candy were his line. His route took him by train and buggy through central Minnesota. He liked the country because it was full of Germans and Swedes. "They are great people for candies," he said.

Sometimes he called on storekeepers and wrote up orders in as many as six small towns in a day. He grew tired of country hotels and bad food. Once he got frostbite, traveling 40 miles by sleigh. "Every one is on the hustle out here," he told his brother in Vermont. "It gets to be tiresome some times, but when one has gotten the fever, it is hard to live in any other way."

Women also earned a living in Minnesota. Most clothing was still made by hand or on home sewing machines. Many women worked at dressmaking, hatmaking, or needlework. Abbie Griffin was one. Her father had died. She and her mother, who was disabled, lived in Minneapolis. In her diary are notes like: "August 15, 1882. Went to town very early and carried two skirts and brought home one more and a pair of velvet slippers to be worked with rosebuds and forget-me-nots." Or: "Thursday, August 24. Still melting hot. Have been at the store all day long. Commenced a table cover. Worked a watch pocket and brought home a skirt to embroider."

Women were beginning to be hired as clerks in dry goods and clothing stores. In 1883 a Minneapolis reporter met a young woman preparing medicines behind the counter in a drugstore. When he looked surprised,

Ojibway women on the Mille Lacs Reservation

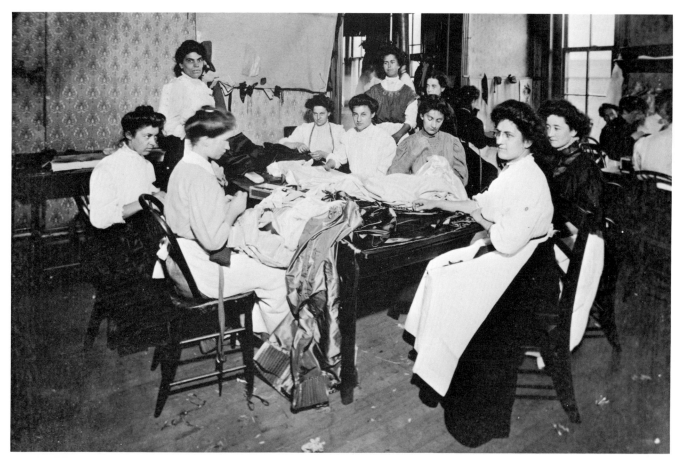

In the 1890s these women worked in the business of a St. Paul dressmaker named Mary Molloy.

she said, "Why shouldn't we? Aren't we as careful as men?" Half a dozen women worked as druggists in the city, she told him, and more were studying pharmacy.

There were plenty of jobs doing housework for others, but most American-born women did not want them. In the 1880s nearly all of the cooks and maids in Minneapolis were immigrants. Two-thirds were Scandinavian and the rest German and Irish. Most earned $3.00 a week and lived in their employers' houses. The usual time off was Sunday afternoon and perhaps one other afternoon or evening.

Immigrants met with many prejudices. According to one woman who ran an employment office: "For cooking and waiting on table the Irish girls are considered best. For general housework, the Germans and Norwegians. There are a great many good Swede girls, but they are not considered so cleanly. All except the Finns are ambitious to learn."

"Religion, Morality, and Knowledge"

The Northwest Ordinance of 1787 had made rules for creating new territories and states. It also called for support of education. "Religion, morality, and knowledge," it said, are needed for "good government and the happiness of mankind." No one had to persuade Minnesota's early leaders that this was true.

The U.S. government gave each new territory some public land for schools. Henry Sibley got Congress to grant Minnesota twice the usual amount. The territory's first legislature passed a law that gave each place

This country school was near Fosston, in northwestern Minnesota, 1895.

with at least five families the right to a school. "Man should be educated for eternity," the law's author declared.

No one knows whether these high-sounding words inspired 17-year-old Anna Lincoln when she chose to be a teacher in 1862. But she was happy to get a job, even at "seven dollars per month and the privilege of boarding around." A country schoolteacher, man or woman, had to be unmarried. The teacher usually lived—or boarded—with the families in the district.

Anna Lincoln's first school was among new settlers in southern Minnesota. It had only 12 pupils and she shared hardships with their families. In one place her bed was in a leaky attic. In another she slept in a room that was used to store corn. She found that "two immense hogs had been killed and brought in and put on the pile of corn and there they were, lying on their backs, feet in the air, frozen stiff, just at the foot of my bed." As life grew easier for farm people, it also improved for country schoolteachers. But most of them moved into a town or looked for other work as soon as possible.

Minnesota hurried to create a university in 1851. But there were few college-level students. It was nearly twenty years before the University of Minnesota held classes. In the meantime, churches were starting schools and colleges. They, too, believed there were connections between religion, morality, and knowledge. By the 1890s there were nine small church-supported colleges. Seven more were added after 1900.

A newspaper office in St. Peter in the 1890s. The editor, John A. Johnson, later became governor of Minnesota.

Maria Sanford came to the University of Minnesota in 1880. The school needed a woman who could serve as advisor for its handful of women students. She also had to teach English and public speaking. The strong-minded, energetic new professor brought these things and many more to the ten-year-old university.

An inspiring public speaker, Maria Sanford was soon teaching people far beyond her classrooms. Minnesotans flocked to hear her lectures on history, art, great books, and travel. She brought the joy of learning and a glimpse of the wider world to churches, civic clubs, teachers' meetings, and farmers' institutes. Some of her university students felt it was too much when she made them come to speech practice at 4:00 A.M. Still, they voted her one of their favorite teachers.

Years later a statue of Professor Sanford was placed in the U.S. Capitol. Beneath it are the words "the best-known and best-loved woman in Minnesota."

Many of the churches behind these colleges were formed by immigrant groups. In the early years Catholics from Germany and Ireland or Lutherans from Norway and Sweden did not worship together. To new immigrants, a church was more than a set of beliefs. It was a place to find their own language and traditions. So Minnesota and the neighboring states had a great number of different churches.

News, Views, Songs, and Stories

Schools and colleges meant people who could read. Minnesota had many of these, so it also had many newspapers. Beginning with the *Minnesota Pioneer* in 1849, more than 5,000 papers were started in the state. Some large towns and cities had daily papers, but most newspapers were published each week in small communities.

Before radio or television, the town paper was the link to what was going on in the world. Early editors did not try to hide their political views. "Republican" or "Democrat" was often part of a newspaper's official name. Besides politics and local news, country papers usually printed poetry and stories by well-known writers. They also had recipes, reports on odd happenings, advice on health care, and whatever else caught the editor's eye.

Minnesota had a few newspapers in languages like German and Swedish. Beginning in 1885 it also had one for black readers, called the *Western Appeal*. This paper started in St. Paul but later had branches in Chicago and other cities. By 1889 it claimed to be "A National

John Ireland served as a Catholic bishop and archbishop in Minnesota from 1875 until his death in 1918. His work to unite the Catholic immigrants from many countries made him one of the best-known leaders of the church in America. He argued that the church must become American just like its members.

Born in Ireland, John came to Minnesota with his parents when he was 14. After studying to be a priest, he served as a chaplain to Minnesota troops in the Civil War. Back in St. Paul, he took a strong stand against the use of liquor. And he worked hard to promote Catholic immigration to the state.

A man of great charm, John Ireland seldom insisted on ceremony. His service in the Civil War had made him an intense patriot. This led him to an interest in civic as well as religious affairs. He had many friends, both Catholic and non-Catholic. Among them were leading Minnesota businessmen, politicians, and educators.

Afro-American Newspaper." In the 1890s black people all over the country read its hard-hitting calls for civil rights and equality.

In other ways, too, Minnesotans reached out to the wider world. Traveling lecturers, musicians, theater companies, balloonists, and circuses got to river towns by steamboat. But until railroads were built, most Minnesotans had to depend on themselves for music, art, entertainment, and sports. Small communities formed baseball teams and played against each other. Sometimes there was horse racing at county fairs. Occasionally a boxing match was held, but respectable people frowned on these.

Families treasured their pianos, violins, and other instruments. Often people got together to play and sing. If they were good enough, they invited others in to listen. People with big houses, like Marion Ramsey Furness, the daughter of Governor Alexander Ramsey, held "musicales" to entertain friends. In St. Paul one "Ladies Musicale" began to meet regularly and took the name Schubert Club. More than a hundred years later it still worked to help local talent and to bring well-known musicians to Minnesota.

A few talented Minnesotans became known beyond the state. Among these were the Andrews family of St. Peter. They formed a "Family Concert and Dramatic Troupe" in the 1870s. Small towns in Minnesota and Iowa welcomed their songs, dances, and comic routines. In the 1880s they started doing light operas and traveled more widely around the Midwest. By the 1890s they performed in eastern cities also.

THE BIG SHOW!
THE
MASTODON
OF THE AGE!
WILL EXHIBIT IN

RED WING,
MONDAY, JULY 29, 1867.

HAIGHT & CHAMBERS'
COLLOSSAL
CIRCUS
AND MENAGERIE!

An advertisement from the Goodhue County Republican

John Q. Adams was shown on the front page when his paper celebrated its 25th anniversary in 1910. By then the newspaper's name had been shortened.

John Q. Adams of St. Paul was the editor and owner of the *Western Appeal.* Through the 1880s and 1890s he led black people in their struggle for justice and civil rights. "No wrongs are ever righted except by protest," he once wrote.

When he came to Minnesota from Louisville, Kentucky, in 1886, Adams already had much experience as an editor and politician. In the Twin Cities he found a small, educated, and well-established community of black people. They read his newspaper and supported him in fighting the spread of segregation during the late 1800s.

Minnesota had a civil rights law. Still, in 1887, a St. Paul hotel refused to rent a room to a black architect. When he protested, he had to spend the night in jail. Adams wrote about it in *The Appeal* and helped to bring a lawsuit against the hotel.

Helping the Poor and the Sick

Like music, drama, and sports, care of the poor and the sick was mainly a do-it-yourself thing. Most counties kept "poor farms." Not only the poor were sent there, but also orphaned, sick, disabled, insane and alcoholic people with nowhere else to go. They were expected to work on the farm. It was a grim place. Being there was thought to be a disgrace, almost like being in jail.

Many churches tried to help the needy. Often a minister turned to the men of the congregation for money. The women gave time and work. In 1867 women from St. Paul's 12 Protestant churches formed an organization of their own "to relieve, aid, and provide homes for the homeless, especially women and children." With rummage sales, ice cream socials, and benefit concerts, they raised money to rent a small house. Later the Home for the Friendless moved to a better building and served for many years. Under another name it became the state's first home for old people.

The sick went to hospitals only when they could not be cared for at home. Most doctors thought hospitals were about the worst places for patients to be. Dr. William Mayo agreed. When a tornado hit Rochester in 1883, many people were hurt. A group of nuns tried to care for them in a

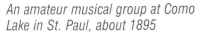

An amateur musical group at Como Lake in St. Paul, about 1895

school. Afterward, Mother Alfred Moes, the head of the group, went to Dr. Mayo. She told him the Sisters of St. Francis would start a hospital if he would be its doctor. At first he said no. But Mother Alfred insisted, and at last he gave in. They called it St. Mary's Hospital. Later it became the headquarters of the famous Mayo Clinic.

In the early years Minnesota boasted about its healthy climate, but contagious disease was common. Smallpox, cholera, and diphtheria were three of the worst killers. No one knew exactly how they spread or what would cure them. When these illnesses appeared, there was often panic.

In the summer of 1868 a steamboat pulled up to the wharf at Red Wing. Pale, scared faces peered over the railings. Word soon got around that there was cholera aboard. Terrified Red Wing people pushed the boat away. They let no one from it come into the town.

Dr. Charles N. Hewitt was new to Red Wing, but he was not new to treating cholera. As an army surgeon, he had seen many soldiers die from it in the Civil War. Quickly he arranged for the boat to unload the sick passengers on an island across the river. There he turned an empty house into an emergency hospital, and the Red Wing town council gave money to care for the victims. The disease did not spread. Hewitt then talked with other doctors. He got them to join him in asking the legislature to create a state board of health. As its head, he spent the next 20 years working to make Minnesota a healthier place.

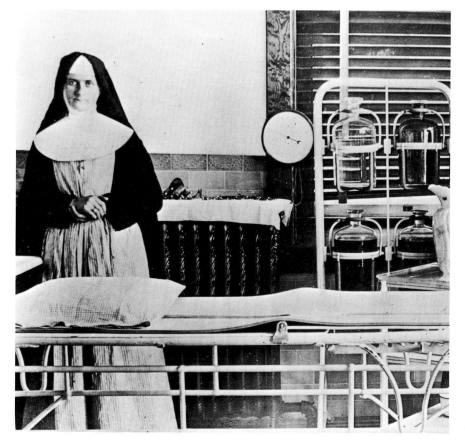

Catholic nuns served as nurses in the St. Mary's Hospital operating room in 1895.

Doctor Martha Ripley came to Minneapolis in 1883. Like other women doctors then, she found that most of her patients were women and young children. In the 1800s most women had babies at home. To those without a home, hospitals gave poor care. And they would not admit a woman who was unmarried. So Dr. Ripley started a new hospital run by women.

Opened in 1887, Maternity Hospital took in any mother who needed care. It soon became known as one of the best and safest places in the Midwest for having a baby. In other ways, too, Martha Ripley spent most of her life trying to help women. She worked hard for the right to vote. She also argued for better family laws and for protection against violence and disease.

Dr. Charles N. Hewitt served as secretary of the state board of health from 1872 to 1897.

This meant telling communities about the need for good sewage treatment and pure drinking water. It meant vaccinating people against smallpox whenever the disease appeared. For other diseases, like diphtheria, it meant quarantine—shutting people in their houses when they became ill and letting no one in or out except those who cared for them.

Charles Hewitt did not live to see new drugs and vaccines wipe out the worst contagious diseases. But by the 1890s Minnesotans had learned to keep them from spreading. Listening to Hewitt and doctors like him, people worked together, used common sense, and avoided panic.

So Minnesota had become safer as well as more comfortable during 40 years of statehood. Measured by the number of schools and churches, knowledge and religion had done well. Thousands of immigrants had found homes and jobs. The fields and forests had produced great wealth. Eighty-year-old Alexander Ramsey could sit on the shaded porch of his stone mansion and think about progress. For him and those like him, Minnesota had kept its promises.

But a new kind of change was in the air. It had already begun in many places. Those who recognized it knew that the next 40 years would transform the state in ways no one could yet foresee.

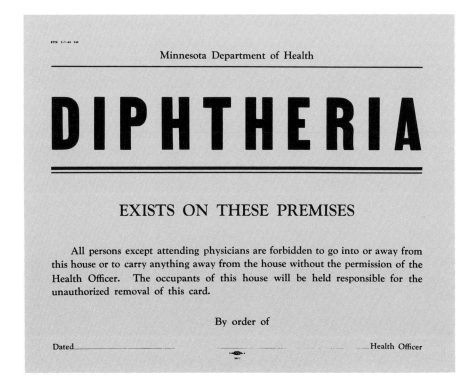

Signs like this were posted on quarantined houses. Diphtheria was a disease of the throat that attacked mostly children. During a deadly epidemic in the 1880s, whole families were wiped out. Some communities in southern Minnesota lost nearly half their children.

Former governor Alexander Ramsey relaxes while his granddaughter, Laura Furness, reads the news, in about 1900.

This advertisement for Minneapolis highlighted railroads and flour mills.

Unit V
Minnesota Joins the Industrial World

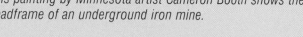

Chapter 15
Machines, Mills, and Mines

A New Era

By the middle of the 1890s the way of living and doing things called industrialism was spreading around the world. The key words of industrialism were *more* and *bigger.* It meant more goods, more money, more jobs, and more people. It meant bigger machines, bigger buildings, and bigger cities. Industrialism brought people more material goods and comfort than ever before. It also made their lives depend on many people they would never see. No longer could you produce for yourself everything you needed to live.

Not only machines and buildings grew bigger. So did the organizations that ran them. Companies that had been owned by one person or by several partners became corporations. A corporation is a make-believe person. It stands in the law for many owners, called stockholders. It was one of the inventions that made industrialism possible.

By forming a corporation and selling stock, businesses could bring together the money of many people. Thus they could buy expensive machinery and build large industries. Soon corporations did business across the country. Like real people, corporations can buy stock. So they can own other corporations. In this way they can be used to make great pyramids of wealth and power.

Industrialism had its roots in the beginnings of modern science, many years earlier. Slowly at first, then faster, inventions changed the way the world looked and how people lived. Some Minnesotans alive in 1890 could remember the first steamboats and trains. They could remember when the first telegraph line reached St. Paul in 1860. They had seen candles replaced by kerosene lamps, then by gas lights. Women had welcomed sewing machines, and food preserved in glass jars and cans. By 1890 some people in cities had telephones. A few had electric lights.

The most important new ideas had to do with power. In 1890 the two main sources of power (except for human muscles) were horses and steam. Trains, ships, and many early factories were run by steam power. But steam engines were big and heavy. For short-distance travel, hauling loads, and farm work, horses still did the job. The invention of the gasoline engine in about 1890 soon changed all this. It was small, simple, light, and very powerful. As years passed, the gas engine made possible cars and trucks, tractors, and airplanes.

This painting by Minnesota artist Cameron Booth shows the headframe of an underground iron mine.

"See the Power There Moving"

Large industry in Minnesota began when lumbermen built sawmills and flour mills beside the Falls of St. Anthony. For years the rushing water turned wheels and spun shafts that moved machinery in mills and factories. In 1869 a Minneapolis citizen wrote some verses about it:

Go with me down to the Falls
And see the power there moving,
Mill stones and saws and countless shafts,
As if 'twere nothing doing.

The mighty river seems to say,
While down the Falls it's pouring:
Use me ten thousand fold as much,
And then I'll not cease roaring.

Only a few weeks later, the falls nearly did stop roaring. Minnesota almost lost its great gift of waterpower. Mill owners who wanted to get even more power tried to dig a tunnel under the falls. One night the tunnel caved in. The river poured through, taking trees, boulders, and buildings. It seemed that the ledge of rock holding up the falls might crumble away altogether.

On October 5, 1869, Minneapolis citizens heard the cry "The falls are going out!" When they rushed to the river, this is what they saw.

Minneapolis people worked hard to plug the tunnel and repair the damage. Then the U.S. government came to the rescue. Over the next 15 years it spent large amounts of money and work to save the waterpower. Workers covered the ledge of rock with a wooden (later cement) "apron" to protect it. Since then many visitors have been puzzled because they cannot see the waterfall they have heard so much about.

During the 1870s flour mills began to push out the lumber mills beside the falls. In 1880 the four blocks on the west bank were crowded with tall stone buildings. Running through canals beneath them, the river's water turned machines that ground wheat into flour. By then Minneapolis produced more flour than any other city in the nation. In 1881 the Pillsbury company opened a new mill across the river on the east side. For a while it was the largest flour mill in the world.

Other industries, too, drew power from the falls. There were cotton and woolen mills, barrel makers, ironworks, and companies that made farm machinery. But as the area filled up, many of these factories, along with the sawmills, moved away from the falls. Steam power let them locate where there was more space. Soon a new way to use the power of the falls gave them freedom to move even farther.

One September evening in 1882, workers at a small plant beside the falls threw a switch. Lights went on in a few bars and stores along Washington Avenue. For the first time in the United States, electricity from waterpower was being sold and sent to users over wires.

The large Minneapolis flour mills replaced many small-town mills like this one advertised in Montevideo.

Steam-powered threshing machines like this were a common sight at harvest time in the late 1800s.

By the 1890s energy from the falls was lighting Minneapolis streets. It had replaced the horses that once pulled streetcars. Electric cars ran farther, and the city spread out. Soon electric elevators made tall buildings possible. So Minneapolis and other cities reached upward also. In a few years electricity would carry telephone and radio messages across the country. Through these invisible networks cities stretched outward in ways never before dreamed of.

"A Farm Is a Factory"

Industrialism was coming to Minnesota farms too. In 1896 the editor of a magazine for farmers wrote bluntly: "A farm is a factory." Farmers, he said, should work by the same rules as other business people. If they could not afford enough land and livestock and machinery to make money, they should sell the farm.

A few readers nodded, many laughed, and some grew angry. Most Minnesota farms were owned and run by families. To them farms were more than just a business. They were homes—places where people as well as plants had deep roots. Farmers or their parents could still remember the lifetime of work it took to turn a prairie homestead into a farm.

When the first gasoline tractors appeared about 1910, no one saw them as the beginning of great change. Tractors worked faster than horses. They did not grow tired and they did not eat. Fields once needed for hay and oats to feed horses could be used for other crops. Still, most farmers kept a team of horses for certain jobs, even when they had a tractor.

Workers on a bonanza farm

Bonanza farms showed Minnesotans what one kind of factory farm was like. These were started by railroad owners and others on the flat plains of the Red River Valley. In the 1870s and 1880s they hired huge crews of men, horses, and machines. They planted and harvested thousands of acres of wheat. The money earned from the first crops was a true bonanza.

A young Norwegian named Knut Hamsun worked on one of the great farms in 1887. Later, back in Norway, he became a famous author. Remembering that summer, Hamsun wrote: "We were called out at three in the morning, when it was still dark. We fed the horses and ourselves and drove the long distance out to the fields, and then day would finally break and we could see what we were about to begin. Not a tree, not a bush grew there— only wheat and grass as far as the eye could see. There was no movement except the swaying of the wheat in the wind; no sound but the chirrup of a million grasshoppers.

"We worked a 16-hour day during the wheat harvest. Ten mowing machines drove after each other in the same field, day after day. When one field was finished, we went to another. And so onward, always onward, while ten men came behind us and shocked the bundles we left. And high on his horse, with a revolver in his pocket and his eye on every man, the foreman sat and watched us. If something went wrong, he was there at once to repair the damage or to order the machine sent back to the yard. He exhausted two horses every day."

At about this time Congress voted money to build up the Agricultural Extension Service. Working through state colleges, the service sent agents into each county. They told farmers how to make more money by using "scientific" methods. Among these were new kinds of crops, new fertilizers, chemicals to kill insects and plant diseases—and, of course, more machinery. To be successful, the agents told farmers, they had to produce more—just as other industries did.

World War I brought high prices. The government urged farmers to help the country win the war by raising more food. Between 1917 and 1919 many bought tractors. With them they could do more work, so they also bought more land. They were caught in the tide of industrialism.

After the war, it turned out that too much food was being raised. Crop prices fell. Yet to make money at low prices, each farmer had to grow even more. Through hard times in the 1920s and 1930s many small farmers gave up. They could not afford the new machines and could not keep going without them. Their fields were taken over by others who could. So, year after year, Minnesota, counted fewer but larger farms.

Meanwhile, jobs like growing seed, making fertilizer, and breeding animals, once done on most farms, became special businesses. So people began to speak of the agriculture industry. They meant not only farmers, but all the businesses linked with farming. Later the word *agribusiness* was invented. It includes companies that make farm machinery, and industries like canning and sugar refining that depend on farm products. The idea of a farm as a food factory no longer seemed strange.

A World War I poster

This style of tractor was common in the 1920s and 1930s. It pulls a machine that cuts wheat and binds it into bundles.

From Horses to Horsepower

The gasoline engine changed Minnesota towns and cities as much as it changed the state's farms. In the 1890s people were trying to attach engines to bicycles, wagons, and buggies. By 1910 Minnesotans had more than 7,000 automobiles. They were not made in factories. Most of them were put together in garages or machine shops. The state had several small companies that built cars.

People liked the new motor buggies, and some of them worked well. But cars could not replace horses until better roads were built. There were no highways. Narrow dirt roads ran from one town to the next. If you were going more than a few miles, you took a train.

The American people, through their government, had made railroads possible by giving the companies land. Next they made automobiles possible by paying taxes to build highways. Minnesota was a leader among the states in doing this. It put a tax on gasoline. The money could be used only to build roads. The state also started a system of numbered highways that the whole country followed.

The network of roads grew, and new factories turned out hundreds of cars. Country people started driving to bigger towns to do their shopping and business. Trains began to pass by the country depots. Then they stopped running on branch lines. In a few years small towns started to shrink. Some of the smallest ones disappeared.

Intercity bus service in this country grew from small beginnings on Minnesota's Iron Range. In 1914 Carl Wickman bought a big touring car. He wanted to sell it, but no one would buy. So his partner, Andrew Anderson, started using it to carry people between the town of Hibbing and a mine location known as Alice.

"Bus Andy" charged 15 cents a ride. Business was so good that he and Wickman soon ordered a real bus. They gave service to other range towns nearby. Then the business moved to Duluth and started statewide bus routes under the name of Greyhound Lines.

Horsepower meets horse on a muddy Minnesota road in the early 1900s. Horsepower is a standard measure of the power produced by an engine. It is the force needed to lift 33,000 pounds one foot in one minute.

162

Cities had already begun to spread. Suburbs had grown up along rail and streetcar lines. With cars, it was easier than ever to move to the edge of town where there was more space. The garage became part of the American home. As people drove hundreds of cars into town each day, they changed the look of downtown areas as well as suburbs.

By the 1940s nearly all main highways were paved. Like older roads, they went through many towns. Still to come were the four-lane interstates that today stretch from city to city and bypass smaller towns. But trucks already were carrying freight that had once been taken by rail. Many passengers were riding buses instead of trains. And some Minnesotans were wondering how much of the state would be covered with tar and cement before the flood of cars stopped.

The Sleeping Giant Wakes Up

The industrial era is often called the age of steel. Bigger buildings and more powerful engines needed stronger materials than brick and wood. Skyscrapers and high bridges had to have steel beams. Steel ships and railroad cars replaced wooden ones. Wagons and buggies made of wood gave way to steel trucks and automobiles. Without Minnesota iron ore, the country's industry might have grown more slowly. From the mines of the Mesabi Range came a large part of the steel that built the nation in the 20th century. It also supplied the weapons for two world wars.

By the early 1930s, hundreds of farm trucks brought cattle
to sell at the stockyards in South St. Paul.

163

Leonidas Merritt

The Merritt family came to Duluth in the 1850s. After the boom of the 1870s ended, Lewis Merritt and his sons found work in the lumber industry. One of the sons was Leonidas, often called Lon. Like Frank Hibbing, the Merritts became experts on timber and also minerals.

Lewis insisted there was iron beneath the ridge of land the Ojibway called Mesabi, or Sleeping Giant. He died in 1880, but his sons remembered. They kept on looking until the ore was found.

Led by Lon, the Merritts formed a mining company. It might have succeeded if hard times had not come in the 1890s. They had to turn to wealthier men for help. Soon they lost control of the company. In a bitter lawsuit against John D. Rockefeller, the Merritts claimed he had cheated them. The jury agreed, but Rockefeller appealed the decision. The appeals court sent the case back to the lower court. Then the Merritts ran out of money. They could fight no further, and a settlement was reached.

Lumber and railroad men had long been sure there was iron in northeastern Minnesota. But no one tried to dig it until 1884. The first mine was at Tower on the Vermilion Range, north and east of the Mesabi. The hard, rocky ore was rich, and people searched for more of it. They expected to find it in deeply buried rock. On the Mesabi they could see only patches of soft, red earth. Most of them gave up and looked elsewhere. One who stayed was Leonidas Merritt.

In 1890 a man who worked for Merritt got a wagon stuck in some red muck. He wondered about its rusty color. At the risk of being laughed at, he took some of the dirt to be tested. It was full of iron. As Merritt later said, "If we had gotten mad and kicked the ground right where we stood, we would have thrown out 64-percent ore." Merritt and his brothers opened a mine there and called it Mountain Iron.

Iron mining needs heavy machinery, many workers, and a cheap way to move tons of ore. Before the mines could make money, railroad tracks had to be laid. Ore-loading docks had to be built. A fleet of ships had to be ready to carry ore across the Great Lakes to steel mills in Pennsylvania and Ohio. It was a job for the rich and powerful, not for small businessmen.

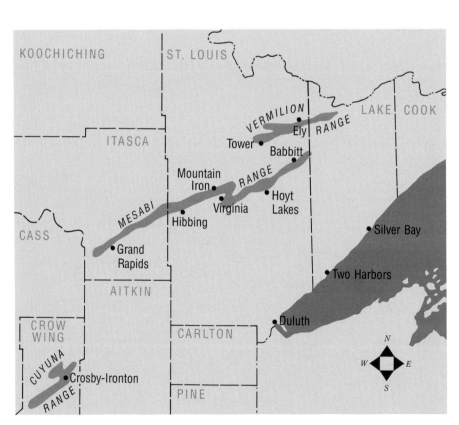

The shaded areas are Minnesota's three iron ranges, the Vermilion, the Mesabi, and the Cuyuna. The Cuyuna Range in Crow Wing County is the smallest and was the last to be discovered. Mining started there in 1911.

Minnesotans found this out in the 1890s. Eastern millionaires like John D. Rockefeller and Andrew Carnegie already controlled most of the iron mines in Wisconsin and Michigan. Soon they added Minnesota, too. Then in 1901 the powerful banker, J. P. Morgan, put together the companies owned by these men and others to make the United States Steel Corporation. The only Minnesotan who still controlled part of the Mesabi was James J. Hill.

Meanwhile mining and lumber had made Duluth into a boom town again. In 1880 it had only 3,500 people. But by 1890 there were nearly ten times that many. During the next 20 years Duluth kept growing. Ore docks crowded the grain elevators and lumber yards on the waterfront. Hundreds of ships steamed through the canal each year. In 1916 a giant steel mill was added. Minnesotans began to realize that their state had a third big city.

At ore docks iron ore was poured from loaded railroad cars into waiting ships. The steamers at left, with rounded sides and top, are called "whalebacks." Duluth ship captain Alexander McDougall designed them to carry ore on the Great Lakes. A shipyard in Superior built many in the 1890s.

J. P. Morgan's United States Steel Corporation was the largest company in the country. Most Minnesotans feared its power. This cartoon from a 1901 Minneapolis paper shows Morgan as an octopus grabbing up many different industries. At the same time a Duluth editor wrote: "The independent miner will soon be a thing of the past." Others warned that workers would be helpless against such a mighty boss.

The corporation was formed to own the stock of other companies important to making steel. It controlled most of the country's iron mines and steel mills. It also had railroads, steamship lines, shipyards, docks, and other kinds of businesses that came along with these.

Chapter 16
The New Cities

City and Country

The changes that came with industrialism reached into every corner of life. People could see it happening first in the growing cities. If they did not like the changes, they often blamed them on city ways. Some Minnesotans may not have been happy about what they saw. Still, they had to admit their state was becoming more urban than rural. By 1920 nearly a third of Minnesota's people lived in the Twin Cities or Duluth.

The cities also reached out to the country in new ways. One was newspapers. By the early 1900s modern printing presses made it possible for newspapers to carry photos. They also could print color. Small-town papers could not afford these things. So before long people all over the state began to read the city papers. Although these might arrive late, they had pictures of the news. They also had colored comic strips and other features that everyone liked.

For more reasons, too, people wanted the city papers. Farmers, bankers, and storekeepers as far west as Montana read the business pages from Minneapolis. Wheat farmers learned about crop prices by reading what was going on at the Minneapolis Grain Exchange. By 1913 banks were part of a new country-wide system called the Federal Reserve. The Federal Reserve Bank for states on the northern plains was in Minneapolis. Storekeepers read the advertisements to learn what goods were new and what city people were buying.

Many of the men who had made money with railroads, flour mills, and lumber companies lived in the Twin Cities. For their families they built fine houses on pleasant streets. They could afford good schools and libraries. Led by people like Thomas B. Walker, a wealthy lumberman who founded the Walker Art Center, they gave money for museums, concerts, and theaters.

As the cities grew, there were more people with education and leisure time to enjoy such things. The Minneapolis (now Minnesota) Symphony Orchestra was formed in 1903. It soon became one of the best orchestras in the Midwest. Minneapolis also became famous for its lovely parks and lakeside drives. In St. Paul, visitors from all around the region gazed at the stately domes of the new capitol and the cathedral. So the Twin Cities became centers for art, architecture, and entertainment.

Robert Koehler's painting of a rainy evening in Minneapolis shows the handsome buildings and well-dressed people seen along Hennepin Avenue around 1910.

But there were darker sides to the growth of cities. One was dishonesty in government. There was much talk about this all over the country in the early 1900s. Cities had become so large that people no longer felt they were in charge of what went on in city hall. In 1902 Minnesotans had to admit that their biggest city no longer had that "Yankee flavor of thrift and soberness" visitors found in 1880. A New York reporter named Lincoln Steffens wrote a book called *The Shame of the Cities*. One chapter told how the mayor of Minneapolis had taken money for protecting gambling and other crimes.

The New Immigration

Some citizens blamed such troubles on the new immigrants crowding into the cities. Minnesota, along with the rest of the country, still received thousands of people from Europe each year. Until the 1890s most immigrants to the state were from northern and western Europe. By the 1900s many of the newcomers came from countries like Italy, Greece, and Poland, in southern and eastern Europe. The state's good farmland was filled up, but its growing industries needed workers. So most of them went to cities or iron mines.

In the cities immigrants took hard, low-paying jobs in mills, packinghouses, and factories. Few understood English and some could not read or write. Many of them lived together in poor areas like Northeast Minneapolis, the West Side of St. Paul, and West Duluth. They spoke their own languages, and to their neighbors they seemed slow in learning American ways.

Dr. Albert A. Ames served as mayor of Minneapolis four times. People liked him and often called him "Doc." He had many friends among the city's poor and unlucky. When they needed a doctor, he helped them. If he knew they could not pay, he forgot how much they owed.

Ames was a tall, handsome, kindly man. He had a way with words, and he loved attention. As he grew older, he spent more time in politics than medicine. But "Doc" also had weaknesses. He drank too much and was easy to wheedle. Doing a friend a favor meant more to him than being honest. He made his brother chief of police. They both took bribes from criminals. Gambling and vice became widespread.

For a long time Minneapolis people tried to look the other way. No one wanted a scandal. They thought it would be bad for the city. But at last the law caught up with Doc Ames. He hurried to get out of the state. His brother and some of his friends went to prison.

In earlier years, when the state had been eager to fill up its prairies and cut down its forests, immigrants had been welcome. But now Minnesotans, along with other Americans, began to wonder how many more were coming. They began to ask whether these strangers really understood ideas like freedom and democracy. Would they blindly follow dishonest politicians and criminal groups? Would they be misled by radical movements that promised them much? Would they still be loyal to some other country?

One way to prevent this was to help the immigrants improve their lives. Another was to teach them the language and laws of their new land. Social settlement houses set out to do these things. Farsighted Minnesotans started places like Pillsbury House in Minneapolis and Neighborhood House on St. Paul's West Side. In spite of these efforts, fear and suspicion of foreigners began to take root in the state.

The New Class of Workers

Civics and English were probably taught in this night school for immigrants held in Eveleth by the Oliver Iron Mining Company.

Another part of city life that made people uneasy was the widening gap between workers and owners. Ever since the coming of French and British fur traders to Minnesota, there had been different social classes. There were bosses and workers, rich and poor. But with the growth of industry, working people in cities felt used by a huge system that cared nothing for them. So they began joining labor unions to demand fair treatment and better wages. Soon people in Minneapolis and St. Paul learned what a strike could mean.

One April day in 1889, Minneapolis streetcar drivers found a notice posted on the door of each carbarn. It told them that wages were being cut. The men had already formed a union, hoping to ask for a raise. They said they could not support families on their low pay. When they learned of the cut, they decided to strike. Drivers turned their horses and headed back for the barns. By early afternoon not a streetcar could be seen. Minneapolis people had to walk home that night. The same thing happened in St. Paul, where the streetcar company was owned by the same man, Thomas Lowry.

When newspaper reporters asked Lowry about the pay cut, he said the company was losing money. "If the men will not work for us at those wages, we will get men who will," he added. The striking drivers answered that the company was making good money. Even then it was planning for new electric car lines in Minneapolis. They asked for arbitration—for some fair outside person to decide the case. Lowry answered: "There will be no arbitration, none whatever." He started hiring new men. Each one had to promise not to join a union.

Not many signed up. The strikers urged other workmen to support them against the "greedy corporation." Their wives got onto the cars and talked new men into quitting. Crowds yelled "scab" as the streetcars went by. People who were tired of walking still refused to ride. Thousands came to public meetings held by the union. In Minneapolis the mayor tried to stop all this by threatening people with arrest and promising to protect the new drivers. But in St. Paul, businessmen told Lowry he should agree to

Thomas Lowry built the Twin City Rapid Transit Company and made himself rich. First he bought the streetcar systems of Minneapolis and of St. Paul. The cars were still pulled by horses, and neither company was making money. But Lowry counted on the future.

The cities were spreading fast. There were no automobiles yet, and streetcars were needed. Soon there would be electric power to run them. In 1891 he formed a new corporation and began to put in electric streetcars. Citizens praised what he was doing for the Twin Cities.

Like many businessmen of his time, Lowry felt that his workers had no rights he did not give them. When they went on strike and asked for arbitration, he was furious. "In future," he huffed, "the Minneapolis Street Railway will run its own business instead of having it run by a union." He and other Minneapolis leaders like him became known for their stand against unions.

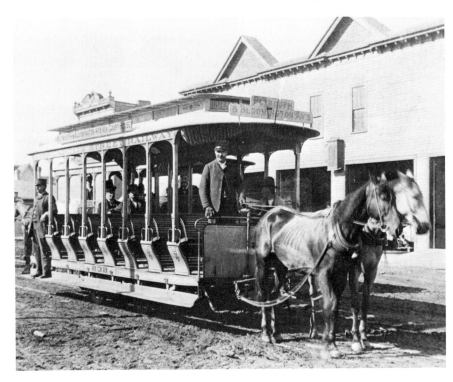

This Minneapolis streetcar ran on the Plymouth and Bloomington Avenue line in 1888. Drivers complained that they had little protection from rain, wind, or cold.

170

A newspaper sketch from the "Easter Riot" in Minneapolis

arbitration. The St. Paul city council talked about taking away his right to run streetcars there.

So many people sided with the strikers that Lowry could not hire enough new drivers. After a few days he sent to Kansas City for nearly a hundred men. Minnesota workers jeered at them. They called them "cowboys," and made fun of the clumsy way they drove streetcars. But the strikers knew they had lost. Not only would they have to work for less money. Many of them would have no jobs at all. On Easter their anger boiled over. Led by a few strikers, Minneapolis crowds blocked the tracks and pushed over two empty streetcars. In St. Paul there was no disturbance.

This first important Minnesota strike showed a difference among communities within the state. Unions spread quietly in St. Paul. There, business owners often treated them as partners in running the workaday world. In Minneapolis and on the Iron Range, companies tried to stamp out unions. Most of the time they succeeded. But the anger this raised among working people led to violence and to calls for radical change.

A New World for Women

Among the new wage earners in city factories were hundreds of young women. Many had come from Minnesota and Dakota farms. They sewed shirts and suits and overalls, flour sacks and mattresses. They wove woolen blankets, made knit underwear, and shaped leather into boots and shoes. They worked in laundries and printshops and made cigars and paper boxes. They also clerked in stores, and some with education and luck found jobs in offices.

This cartoon appeared in a labor paper called Solidarity *in 1916. The figure of a worker with a club stands for the Industrial Workers of the World (IWW). The radical labor organization led a miners' strike on the Iron Range that year.*

A poster for woman suffrage

Those who had families in the city lived at home. But in the early 1900s Minneapolis had more working women living in rented rooms than most other cities. To many people this was shocking and unnatural. They worried that women living away from parents or husbands would be victims of crime and vice.

The life of a "factory girl" was not easy. Most of them were not paid for the time they worked but for the number of pieces they finished. The money was so little that only by working very fast could they earn enough to buy food and pay rent. The usual day was ten hours—from 7:00 A.M. to 6:00 P.M., with an hour off for lunch. The places they worked were often dark, stuffy, and badly heated. In one Minneapolis bag factory a visitor found the air so thick with dust and lint she could hardly see. "You have to get used to the dust," one of the women told her. "Some of the girls can't stand it at all and have to leave." In a few places they joined unions, but most were too afraid of losing their jobs.

Minnesota women had been asking for the right to vote (suffrage) since the founding of the state, with little success. By 1900 they could vote only for the members of school and library boards. Opponents argued that women were homemakers, supported and protected by men, so they needed no part in making laws. As more women began working in factories and offices, this became harder to believe.

Each time the Minnesota legislature met, women brought up the subject. They pointed to other states, like Wyoming, that already had

Clara Hampson Ueland was one of many Minnesota women who worked long and hard for the right to vote. Some others were Harriet Bishop, Jane Grey Swisshelm, Maria Sanford, and Dr. Martha Ripley. Like most of them, Clara Hampson was well educated. Before her marriage to Minneapolis lawyer Andreas Ueland, she taught school.

For years women had said that it was only fair for them to help make the laws they had to obey. As president of the Minnesota Woman Suffrage Association in 1914, Clara Ueland used some new arguments. "Mothers, from the beginning," she wrote, "have been the force that makes for better homes and higher civilization. This concern for home should be expressed in government." She went on to say that women voters would help to clean up politics. The idea impressed people who were worried about dishonesty in government.

woman suffrage. But still the lawmakers refused. At last in 1919 the state allowed women to vote for president. A year later an amendment to the U.S. Constitution gave all American women the same voting rights as men.

New Roles for Government

One strong argument for giving women a voice in government was that government itself was changing. It had to grow along with growing cities and industries. In an industrial world people had less control over their lives. They needed protection, and they turned to government. It affected homes and families more than ever before. Its services and rules began to touch men, women, and children each day.

When most of the things people bought were made by their neighbors, they already knew the quality of the goods. As industries and trade grew, that was no longer true. They demanded that government inspect foods and medicines to be sure these were pure and safe. Other products, too, had to be tested to protect people from dangers they had no way to know about.

In large cities everyone depends on having water, electricity, telephones, and streetcars or buses. Those services are called public utilities. They cannot be stopped just because they are losing money. Government has to make sure that they are run properly and keep on serving people honestly. Sometimes it owns them. Sometimes it supervises the private companies that do.

These Stillwater women exercised their right to vote for the first time in a general election, in 1920.

With the coming of cars, someone also had to build roads and highways and see that traffic rules were obeyed. This task alone made city, county, and state governments grow immensely. Such growth meant more and bigger office buildings, higher taxes, and, above all, new workers. As the 20th century moved along, more and more people found jobs with the government.

Other kinds of systems, too, were beginning to need government rules. Banking and insurance services were important to industry. When they failed, thousands of workers were thrown out of jobs. People demanded that government prevent this. The difference in power between workers and corporations brought still more needs. Heavy machinery in factories and mines often killed and injured workers. Employers did not think they were responsible for such accidents. So government provided insurance called worker's compensation to help injured workers pay their bills. Also adopted as time went on were rules about child labor, unhealthy work places, and pay too low to live on.

With all these new tasks and powers, government seemed more important. Citizens were no longer willing to leave it to political parties. They wanted more to say about how it was run. In Minnesota, new laws let voters instead of party meetings choose party candidates. (This is called a direct primary.) They also made many offices nonpartisan—not chosen by political party. The idea was that voters should just elect good people for

These St. Paul office workers were among many women sitting at desks and typewriters in 1911.

certain offices. Judges could be wise and fair whether they were Democrats or Republicans. City mayors could be honest and run city business carefully no matter what their political party.

The most unusual step Minnesotans took was to make their state legislature nonpartisan. The experiment, started in 1913, did not work. Passing laws is not a nonpartisan task. Candidates did not have to say what party they favored. But after they were elected, they formed groups (called caucuses) that were much the same as parties. As years passed, voters decided that some of the new rules adopted early in the 20th century should be changed back again. Minnesota's nonpartisan legislature was dropped in 1973.

Thomas Van Lear became mayor of Minneapolis after the office was made nonpartisan. In earlier years only a Democrat or a Republican could have been elected. Van Lear was neither. He belonged to the Socialist party. But under the new Minnesota law, mayors were not chosen by party. According to one newspaper, Van Lear was "well known as a man who cared little for a party name but everything for principles."

After their bad experience with Mayor Ames, Minneapolis voters wanted honest city government. In 1916 they feared that powerful public utilities like the streetcar and electric companies were getting unfair favors. They wanted a mayor who would not be bribed or pushed around.

Workers especially liked Van Lear. He was the leader of a union. He promised he would not use the police to help break strikes as several Minneapolis mayors had done. Van Lear kept the promise. In 1918 business people worked hard to defeat him. He lost by a few votes.

One problem of government in growing cities was keeping the streets clean. In 1904 St. Paul street sweepers paraded down Sixth Street.

Chapter 17
World War I

Shadows of Change

For Minnesotans, like most Americans, the first 15 years of the 20th century was a period of excitement and hope. Times were good. Farmers got good prices for their crops, and people had jobs. There were many things to buy if you had money—cars, cameras, record players, typewriters, and dozens of other new gadgets. City folk looked at them in stores. On farms people saw them in mail order catalogs.

Like other government services, mail delivery had grown. Most farmers no longer went to town to pick up letters and packages. Now they could have things sent to their own gates. And big new mail order companies like Sears, Roebuck and Montgomery Ward would send anything from hats to horse harnesses.

During the day people talked proudly of progress. But sometimes they lay awake at night worrying over the changes they saw. Who was really running the country—or might be planning to? People read reports about dishonest politicians, special interests, and radical plots. There were also deep questions over how far government should go in running the lives of people.

One such question was prohibition. This meant stopping the sale of liquor. Many Minnesotans favored it. Others were outraged. In the end Minnesota voted for it. The U.S. Constitution was amended in 1919 to allow the ban on liquor. Then a law had to be written. One of the state's congressmen, Andrew Volstead, headed the right committee. So the job went to him, and the law became known as the Volstead Act. He was surprised to find that people thought of him as Mr. Prohibition. "I never made a prohibition speech in my life," he once said.

So Minnesotans struggled over issues like the power of giant corporations, corruption in cities, unions, woman suffrage, and prohibition. They paid little attention to what was happening in Europe. War started there in 1914 between the Allies (England and France) and the Central Powers (Germany and Austria). It seemed far away from Minnesota.

In 1916 many Minnesotans voted for President Woodrow Wilson. His supporters boasted that "he kept us out of war." But it was already becoming clear that he would not do so much longer. People across the country were beginning to think that the future of world peace and democracy lay with the Allies. Anger at Germany grew stronger each day. It increased

This picture is from a World War I poster urging people to buy government liberty bonds. It shows an American warship defending an ocean liner against a German submarine.

when German submarines sank American ships and stories were printed of cruelty by German soldiers. (Most of these proved to be false.) Early in April 1917, the United States declared war. Suddenly the whole country was in a fever of patriotism.

A Soldier from Barnesville

Each state had sent its own troops to the Civil War. In World War I most of the 126,000 Minnesotans who served were mixed in with military units from all over the country. One exception was a Minnesota National Guard regiment called the 151st Field Artillery. All of its members were Minnesotans. It fought through many bloody battles on the western front, between France and Germany. To the state's people the heroic record of this unit stood for Minnesota's part in the war.

One member of the 151st was Corporal Maurice Masterson. He was from Barnesville, just south of Hawley in the Red River Valley. In the spring of 1917 he was studying at the University of Minnesota. Popular and talented, he had just been elected editor of the college yearbook. When the war started he volunteered at once.

After only a week in France, Maurice wrote to his mother: "Before I left the U.S. I felt glad of the chance to strike a blow in defense of humanity. Since I arrived my heart is filled with regret that I did not come before. I am beginning to see what these people have suffered." Like many Ameri-

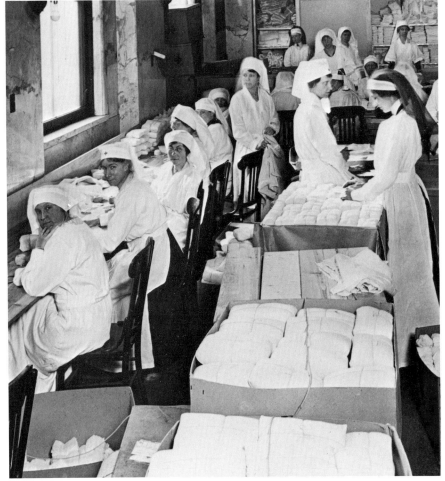

In World War I the Red Cross became a symbol of the active role of women as army nurses, war workers, and patriots. Here St. Paul Red Cross volunteers fold bandages.

178

cans, he believed that if Germany won, the war would soon reach the United States. "I would rather die a thousand times," he said, "than have you or any American mother living under the terrible shadow of war at home." A few days later he told her they would not be in action for a while. "When we are—well, it's all in the game, just a part of the price of war if some of us don't come back."

By April 1918 Maurice was in the trenches, wishing it were over. "If the men who make war had to go to the front as common soldiers," he wrote, "there would be an end of all war. And it's not the danger. It's the eternal dirt, the lice, the cold, the mud." But he could still laugh at how he looked: "My hat is a steel helmet made in bowl shape. My hair is not often neatly trimmed, but I am at all times cleanly shaved for the reason that my gas mask must fit tightly on my face. Of course I wear a moustache, oh a charming red affair."

A month later he promised to tell his family "a thousand tales of human nature" when he got home. "War," he said, "soils everything it touches save the men who fight the war." Early in October, as the Allied armies pressed forward, he was sent to a hospital with poison gas and shell shock. Two weeks later he went back to the front, decorated for bravery. On November 11, 1918, the war ended. The Mastersons, like thousands of parents everywhere, breathed a thankful prayer. A few days later they got a telegram. Maurice had been killed on November 1.

Poison gas was one of the terrible new weapons first used in World War I. These Minnesota soldiers wear gas masks for protection.

Opponents of War

Not all Minnesotans believed there was a need to fight Germany. Some felt that England and France were just as much at fault for the war. They had protested against U.S. businesses selling weapons to the Allies. Early in 1916 a German-American farmer from Faribault County wrote to Senator Knute Nelson: "It is a shame that we have people in Washington that go to church on Sunday and pray for peace and the next day they are in favor to sell more ammunition to kill people."

One of the strongest Minnesota voices against the sale of arms was Congressman Charles A. Lindbergh from Little Falls. "The manufacture for export of war material and death-dealing instruments is a crime against humanity," he said. He urged Congress to forbid it. Lindbergh hoped to run for the U.S. Senate in 1916. His party chose Frank B. Kellogg instead. Kellogg also said he was against war. But he felt the best way to stay out was being prepared to fight.

After war was declared, nearly everyone agreed they must support the country. But in Minnesota there were thousands who had come from Germany. Many still had friends and families there. It was hard for them to believe President Wilson when he said the war was against the German government, not its people. In Minnesota most schools stopped teaching the German language. State officials examined schoolbooks to be sure they did not praise Germany. Even sermons preached in German were said to be un-American. It hurt immigrants to hear their homeland called "the German Beast" and its people "man-eating Huns."

Frank B. Kellogg was a well-known St. Paul lawyer. Some of the country's leading Republicans were his friends. As a senator, Kellogg voted to declare war on Germany. He was one of many who thought World War I had to be fought to stop war forever.

When Kellogg's term ended, the war was over. Food prices had fallen. Minnesota farmers were in deep trouble. They were angry and voted for the new Farmer-Labor party. Kellogg lost the election. But in Washington the Republicans were in power. They made him ambassador to England and later secretary of state.

All through his life Kellogg kept on working for world peace. He spent his last years as a judge on the World Court, which had been created as part of the League of Nations.

Denying American Liberties

Huns *was a favorite word with pro-war writers and speakers. It compared Germans to a barbarian people called Huns who invaded Europe at the end of Roman times.*

When Congress passed a draft law, German-Americans became deeply worried. They were willing to defend the United States. But many did not want to fight for England and France against Germany. They pointed out that Americans had never been drafted to make war in a foreign country. And they argued that it was against the U.S. Constitution.

Early in the summer of 1917 German-Americans in New Ulm held a meeting to discuss these questions. It was a peaceful meeting. The speakers talked of their loyalty to the United States and obeying the law. But they agreed to ask the government not to send young men overseas to fight against their own kinfolk. Soon New Ulm faced a storm of anger. When the governor learned of the meeting, he removed the town's mayor from office. Those at the meeting were said to be resisting the draft. Newspapers all over the state called the people of New Ulm traitors.

The fear of disloyalty and treason did not stop at German-Americans. It spread through Minnesota like a deadly disease. Wartime turned the worries that had haunted people for years into outright panic.

The Minnesota legislature created a Commission of Public Safety. It had power to do almost anything to support the nation. The commission claimed that strikes and labor protests blocked the war effort. It formed a Home Guard of men too old for the regular army. The guard was used to keep peace and break strikes.

181

Another task of the commission was to keep watch over certain organizations. One was the Industrial Workers of the World (IWW). This labor group had many members among Minnesota miners and lumberjacks. Another was the Nonpartisan League, a political movement of North Dakota and Minnesota farmers. They were much like earlier Grangers and Populists. The farmers supported the war, but they asked the government to draft money as well as men. They demanded a limit on business profits so rich people would not grow richer from the war. For that they were called disloyal.

The commission's example led people all over the state to watch their neighbors for signs of disloyalty. Sometimes they got together to punish "traitors." No one stopped them. There was bullying and mob violence. For more than a year freedom of speech disappeared in Minnesota.

Suspicion of foreigners also went beyond German-Americans. Everyone in the state who was not a citizen had to register with the Commission of Public Safety. There was a great drive to "Americanize" immigrants. Speaking any language but English was thought unpatriotic—in churches, in schools, and in meetings. Even words like *Swedish-American* or *Irish-American* were frowned on. Everyone, immigrants were told, was just an American and should be proud of it. All the ways and memories of old homelands should be forgotten as soon as possible. No one had a right to be different.

Charles A. Lindbergh is often called "senior" to tell him from his more famous son. His parents were Swedish immigrants. He grew up on a frontier farm and became a lawyer in the town of Little Falls.

Lindbergh felt the country's banking system was run by a few powerful people like J. P. Morgan. In a book he wrote he called them "The Money Trust." He blamed them for pushing the country into war with Germany.

In 1918 the Nonpartisan League backed Lindbergh for governor. The war was going on. His opponents claimed both Lindbergh and the Nonpartisan League were traitors.

During the campaign Lindbergh ran many risks. He was shot at, threatened by mobs, and arrested. Stones, rotten eggs, and yellow paint were thrown. Straw dummies of him were hanged. Nineteen Minnesota counties forbade the Nonpartisan League to hold public meetings. Other places, like Duluth, found ways to keep him from speaking. Despite this, he had loyal friends among farmers and workers.

The votes of Lindbergh supporters like these were not enough to win the election in 1918.

Afterward

Anne and Charles Lindbergh

Charles A. Lindbergh Jr. was 16 years old when his father ran for governor in 1918. He was more interested then in cars and motorcycles than in politics. Later he turned to planes and became a pilot. In 1927 he was the first flyer to cross the Atlantic Ocean nonstop and alone. The daring flight made him a national hero. For a while he was the best-known Minnesotan in the world.

Young Lindbergh continued flying. With his wife, Anne Morrow Lindbergh, he test flew world airline routes. Their work helped give people confidence in air travel. Although he never ran for office, he did speak for U.S. neutrality in World War II. This made him unpopular with many people. Some said he favored Hitler. Lindbergh denied this. During the war, he served as a test pilot for U.S. planes and flew many dangerous missions. In later years he spoke out for saving the environment.

For America, World War I lasted only a year and a half. After the soldiers were welcomed home, everyone tried to get back to life as it had been before. But the world had changed. In Minnesota the memory of abuse and injustice lasted a long time. It made workers, farmers, and many immigrants stick together.

The Nonpartisan League disappeared, but its supporters joined with union people to form a new Farmer-Labor party. Before long it was one of Minnesota's two major parties. The Democrats, who had never been strong in the state, became a weak third party.

During the 1920s and 1930s there was much antiwar feeling. Minnesotans were proud when their former senator, Frank Kellogg, became U.S. secretary of state. In 1928 he helped get the world powers to promise never to make war again. For that agreement—called the Kellogg Pact—he was given the Nobel Peace Prize.

But the pact turned out to be empty words for the nations that had signed it. By the middle of the 1930s Europe was again preparing for war. Germany this time was led by Adolf Hitler. It threatened England and France with even greater danger than in World War I. Once more Americans were faced with the question of how much to help the Allies.

In Minnesota the answer was clear. The state's popular Farmer-Labor governor, Floyd B. Olson, said "I wouldn't trade the life of one youth for the whole damned 'freedom of the seas.' If we want to keep out of war, we should sell nothing to a combatant." As Hitler grew stronger, some disagreed. But many Minnesotans still hoped for U.S. neutrality.

Young Minneapolis peace demonstrators in 1936

Unit VI
Minnesota in Midcentury
—Not so Long Ago

Chapter 18
Depression on the Farms and in the Cities

Minnesota in the 1920s

To many Minnesotans in the 1920s their state looked the same as before World War I, yet somehow it had changed. Big city ways had come to stay. For the first time, many ordinary people could buy a car. And roads were good enough to get them places. Moving pictures were still silent, but most up-and-coming towns had a theater. Across the state people laughed at Charlie Chaplin and sighed over Mary Pickford. Some also listened to radios. Commercial radio started in 1922. That year nine stations went on the air in Minnesota.

City people with money and cars were discovering the lakes and pines of northern Minnesota. They stayed at resorts and built summer cabins. Going to the lake was becoming a part of Minnesota life for more than a few rich folk. At the same time people began to think about saving the trees and unspoiled places that were left. People who urged this were called conservationists. It was a new word in Minnesota.

The lives of women had changed. Many who had taken wartime jobs in factories and offices stayed on. Skirts were short and so was hair. Now women could vote. In 1922 Anna Dickie Olesen was the Democratic candidate for the U.S. Senate. People crowded to hear her. If they came to laugh, they often went away thinking about what she had said. Minnesotans did not elect her, but they did send four women to the state legislature that year.

In northern Minnesota and in the cities there were plenty of jobs. Iron mines and factories were busy. In forest areas new paper mills made use of trees not good for lumber. Around lakes the tourist business was growing. In the rest of the state it was different. The farm depression that started just after the war kept on through the 1920s. Prices for crops stayed low. The price of everything else was high.

Through the 1920s most farmers still did without electric lights, running water, and central heat. In cities, suburbs, and many small towns, the building of power plants, gas lines, and water systems became a growing industry. A few businessmen had the idea of tying such public utilities into large groups. One was Wilbur Foshay. Big systems, he argued, work better than small ones. They can borrow more money and hire more experts. He built a pyramid of corporations with the Foshay Company at the top. The

Artist Edwin Nooleen caught a common depression-era scene when he painted these jobless men in Minneapolis. Others are lined up outside an employment office across the street.

A 1920s radio

Grim Times

bottom was a network of small gas, electric, and water companies all across the country. His profits came mostly from selling stock. As long as people kept buying, the scheme worked.

In 1927 Foshay decided on a new building in Minneapolis. As a boy he had admired the Washington Monument. He told the architects to design a tower like it. It was to be the finest and tallest in the city. When it was finished in the fall of 1929, Foshay held a three-day celebration. Hundreds of important visitors came. Speeches were given. The world-famous band of John Philip Sousa played for the event. Everyone admired the building with FOSHAY in huge letters across the top.

A few days later the stock market crashed. The whole country headed into depression. Foshay's business pyramid crashed, too. By November he was broke. So were many people who had bought stock from him. Later Foshay was sent to prison for fraud. But the tower he had built would stand proudly above the Minneapolis skyline for many years.

During the same fall a young black man named Gordon Parks worked as a waiter at St. Paul's exclusive Minnesota Club. Customers talked in hushed voices about the stock market. But Parks thought it "surely concerned only the rich." Then he was laid off. He recalled that soon "hard times had settled in. My kinfolk had, like many others, lost their jobs and their credit. They were just hang-

For more than forty years the Foshay Tower was the tallest building in Minneapolis.

ing on. I had given up my room on my birthday, owing a month's rent, promising my landlady I would pay. Now the days would be spent searching for work and going from one relative to another to sleep or, if there was enough food, to eat."

Black people were not the only ones to suffer. In Duluth "a lot of people lost everything," according to one salesman. His pay was cut. His wife remembered: "We had a garden we depended on. We canned vegetables and picked raspberries and apples. The children had to help, too. The boys had paper routes. Our daughter peddled raspberries down the block to our neighbors. I'd buy a pot roast and it would have to last all week in one form or another." Like many other women, she tried to help support the family by finding work. But the few jobs open were often reserved for men.

On the Iron Range a miner recalled: "We found ourselves working five days a week instead of six, and then four days a week, and then four days every other week. We reached the lowest in 1932, when we worked about three days a month for six months. Then for six months we had no work at all."

On top of the troubles they already had, farmers on the Great Plains were hit by a terrible drought. It lasted for five years, from 1931 through 1936. In western Minnesota and the Dakotas crops died. Grasshoppers finished whatever was left. Dust storms darkened the sky in the Twin Cities. Yet the prices paid to farmers were lower than ever.

Hannah Kempfer was one of four women elected to the legislature in 1922. She was from Otter Tail County. The other three were from Minneapolis. Hannah had come to Minnesota from Norway when she was six. Her family was poor, and she had to work hard, even as a child. Still, she managed to finish school and become a country teacher.

Although as a girl she had hunted and trapped animals to earn money, she loved wild creatures. In her 18 years as a legislator, she became known for support of conservation and of laws to regulate hunting and fishing. This was not always popular. Her only defeat in an election came after she sponsored a law that made state citizens get fishing licenses.

Gordon Parks came to Minnesota from Kansas when he was 16. His mother had died and his family had scattered. Through the depression he worked at odd jobs and tried to finish school in St. Paul. For a few weeks one winter he had no place to stay. He slept on Twin Cities streetcars. After a year at a CCC camp he got a job as a waiter on trains from Minneapolis to Seattle.

One day he bought a secondhand camera. From then on he knew he would be a photographer. In time he became famous—not only for his pictures but also for articles and books. One book, called *A Choice of Weapons,* is the story of his hard years growing up in the depression.

One Nobles County man who began farming in 1929 said: "There was a lot of guys started same year I did that didn't make it. Guys that I knew, that I grew up with. A lot of them borrowed a lot of money, and when things got rough, why, the bank had to have the money, and they sold 'em out. That's all there was to it."

Desperate for help, people turned to the government. In 1930 Minnesota voters elected a Farmer-Labor governor named Floyd B. Olson. He got votes from many who were not members of his party. Most of the same people voted for Democrat Franklin D. Roosevelt as president in 1932. Roosevelt promised the country a "New Deal."

Farmers Take a Holiday

Farmers in the Upper Midwest formed the Farmers Holiday Association in 1932. The aim was to keep food from getting to markets until farm prices rose. As one Iowa member wrote:

Let's call a Farmers' Holiday
A Holiday let's hold
We'll eat our wheat and ham and eggs
And let them eat their gold.

Not only did they keep their own produce. They also set up roadblocks to keep other farmers from selling theirs. Trucks carrying cattle,

Prohibition ended in 1933. This Minneapolis beer truck was ready to roll on the day the law changed.

hogs, milk, and other food into towns had to turn back. Sheriffs and police called it a strike, not a holiday. They tried to stop the protesters. In some states people were hurt and killed in the rioting that followed. This kind of action made headlines. But it did not gain much for farmers.

The Holiday Association was strong in Minnesota. But the farm strike brought little violence to the state. John Bosch, who led the organization in Minnesota, recalled, "It didn't take long to see that we were getting nowhere with the strike." There were better ways to help farmers, he thought.

One way was to keep farms from being sold for unpaid debts. (This is called foreclosure.) The Holiday Association stopped many foreclosure sales. When the leaders learned someone was going to lose a farm, they sent out word. Hundreds of farmers came. One sale in Willmar drew nearly a thousand people.

First Bosch always tried to stop a sale by talking with the sheriff. Sometimes it worked. Most people wanted to help farmers if they could. At Willmar the sheriff said, "I've sworn to uphold the law, and I've got to do it." Bosch recalled: "I had made arrangements with eight powerful men, two for each arm and two for each leg. And when the hour came and I couldn't convince him, the next second he was flat on his back on the floor. And he stayed there."

John H. Bosch grew up in west central Minnesota. His parents taught him politics along with farming. When he was only three, a visitor asked his name. "I'm a Populist," he answered proudly. He never went to high school, but he read many books and was a well-educated man.

Among the books were some about the spiritual leader in India, Mohandas Gandhi. Bosch was deeply impressed by Gandhi's idea of resisting unjust laws without violence. As president of the Minnesota Holiday Association he tried to do the same. Thus he avoided battles between angry farmers and police.

This western Minnesota farmer in the 1930s showed what the drought had done to his land.

What farmers really wanted was a law to stop foreclosures until times were better. Then they could earn money to pay their debts. In February 1933, Governor Olson declared an emergency. He stopped all such sales in Minnesota and asked the legislature to pass a law. While the lawmakers debated, thousands of farmers marched to the Capitol. On May 1 the law they asked for was passed.

Workers Go on Strike

Through the 1920s not many Minnesota workers joined unions. In the cities, in the iron mines, and in the lumber camps their strikes had been broken and their leaders jailed during World War I. After the war, companies hired labor spies. Anyone who tried to form a union was reported and quickly fired. In Minneapolis employers joined a group called the Citizens Alliance. Its leaders firmly believed that unions were un-American. By the 1930s wages in Minneapolis were below those in most other cities.

The depression years saw a new wave of strikes. In 1933 meatpackers at the Hormel Company in Austin called the state's first "sit-down" strike. They not only quit work. They also stayed in the plant to keep new workers from taking their places. The company asked the governor to send the National Guard and make the strikers leave. Olson refused. Finally the company agreed to arbitration.

In 1934, the eyes of the whole country turned to Minneapolis. Headlines told of "civil war" in the streets. It started in May with a strike by the

Protesting farmers in St. Paul, 1933

190

city's truck drivers. They wanted more pay. But the real fight was about the union's right to speak for all employees of trucking companies. Hundreds of strikers walked the streets. They stopped trucks and shut down gas stations. Other workers and many people without jobs helped the strikers. Business in Minneapolis came to a stop. Still the companies, supported by the Citizens Alliance, refused to bargain with the union.

City police guarded trucks, but there were not enough police. So businessmen organized a "citizens army." Those who joined became police deputies. They tried to protect convoys of trucks moving through the city. Crowds of strikers met them. Both sides were armed with clubs and bricks. Each day the fights grew worse. On May 22 a battle lasted for several hours. Two people were killed and hundreds hurt.

After that there was a short truce. Federal and state officials tried hard to work out a compromise. But on the key question of one union for all workers in the trucking industry, the companies would not budge. In July the strike started again. This time the police used guns. One day two strikers were killed and more than sixty wounded as they tried to run. The city was horrified. The governor put Minneapolis under martial law.

Meanwhile federal officials, directed by President Roosevelt, were quietly putting pressure on members of the Citizens Alliance. Among them were large banks that owed the government money. The business leaders of the city realized they could no longer keep Minneapolis a non-union

Under martial law, these national guard troops took the place of police in Minneapolis during the summer of 1934.

Floyd B. Olson is one of Minnesota's best-remembered governors. For six years during the worst of the depression he led a deeply divided state. He had a way of making people feel he was on their side, even when they did not agree with his ideas.

A tall, rugged-looking man, Olson had a Norwegian father and a Swedish mother. He grew up in a poor neighborhood of Minneapolis. His firsthand knowledge of poverty and working people drew him to the Farmer-Labor party. As its leader, he called for many changes in the state and nation. But as governor, he was usually practical and cautious.

Politicians across the country shook their heads over Minnesota. It was neither Democratic nor Republican and it had a nonpartisan legislature! In 1934 they saw Olson reelected against heavy odds. Many predicted that he and the Farmer-Labor party would move into national politics. Then in 1936 Floyd Olson died of cancer.

town. Most smaller employers had long since grown tired of the struggle. So at last the bosses signed a contract with the union.

The truckers' strike was a turning point for labor in Minnesota. Along with other strikes across the country, it showed the need for new laws. In 1935 Congress passed the National Labor Relations Act. This set standards of fairness to unions and rules for bargaining between employers and workers. Unions grew. In 1937 the mighty United States Steel Corporation agreed to bargain with its workers. Soon miners on Minnesota's iron ranges were able to join the United Steelworkers without fear of losing their jobs.

Indians Reorganize

For Minnesota's Ojibway people, the depression was not much worse than the hard times they usually had. They lived by gardening, fishing, and gathering wild rice. Sometimes they found work at logging or farm labor. There were never enough jobs, and wages were low. Their houses were small, old, and crowded. Sickness was widespread. Not until 1924 did Indians have the right to vote. Even that did not change the poverty and oppression under which they lived.

In 1933 they, too, got a New Deal. First came the Civilian Conservation Corps (CCC). It was one of many government plans to create jobs. Under the CCC young men lived at army-type camps in forest and desert areas. There they did conservation work.

An Indian CCC crew planting young trees on the Nett Lake Reservation

In Minnesota the CCC gave Indian people much-needed jobs. Special rules were made to let them stay at home. They could build roads, plant trees, fight forest fires, and improve campgrounds on their own reservations. One Indian CCC camp was at Nett Lake. "Last July," wrote a foreman, "brown army tents sprang up overnight like toadstools. Later the tents gave place to 14 neat buildings of freshly cut pine from the Red Lake Indian sawmill. Everywhere is bustling activity. All day and half the night trucks loaded with men and supplies roar in and out of camp."

Along with the jobs, the New Deal brought new respect for Indian ways. No longer were Indians forbidden to hold traditional religious ceremonies or speak their own languages. The government also tried to help tribal people organize. Until the 1930s few Indian groups had their own local governments, although some had formed tribal councils. One such council was on Minnesota's Red Lake Reservation.

In 1934 Congress passed the Indian Reorganization Act. It set up guidelines for writing constitutions and electing officers along the lines of a white government. Not all Indians thought this was a good idea. But most felt that it would give them more power to defend their rights. In 1936 six Minnesota Ojibway reservations (all but Red Lake) joined the Minnesota Chippewa Tribe. Each reservation picks its own business committee. These elect officers for the whole tribe. Later four small Dakota communities organized separately in the southern part of the state. With tribal governments, Minnesota Indians began to have more voice in the state. They spoke out, and others had to listen.

Emblem of the federal conservation program's Indian division. The CCC was one of many New Deal "alphabet" agencies, known by their initials. Another was WPA.

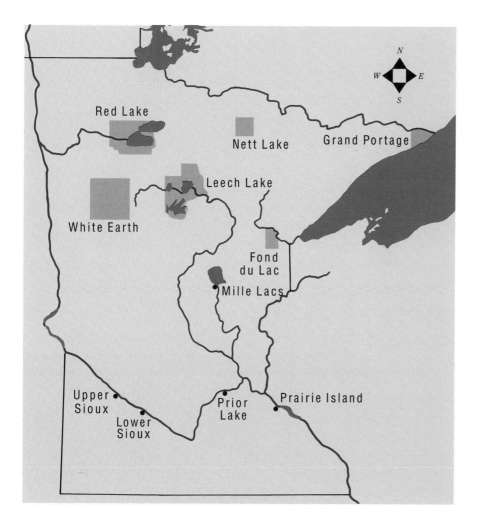

Minnesota's Indian reservations seem large on this map. Only at Red Lake is all the land owned by Indians. On others, as much as three quarters of the reservation belongs to white people.

Chapter 19
World War II and After

One World

For Minnesota, World War II was very different from World War I. Germany, Italy, and Japan were foes of the United States. But this time there was little backlash against German people or any others in the state. When the U.S. government forced all Japanese-Americans to leave their homes on the West Coast, some moved to Minnesota. Here they found less prejudice and distrust than in western states.

Unlike the first world war, the second lasted four years, from 1941 to 1945. As before, Minnesota men and women served in the armed forces with other Americans. They saw action throughout the world. Some did not come back.

At home the war caused shortages of many things. Gasoline, sugar, and other goods were rationed. Minnesota farmers grew record crops to feed armies and people in war-torn countries. Miners dug more iron than ever before. Plants in the cities were busy day and night. They turned out guns, ammunition, bombs, and other war materials. But while everyone worked for victory, high-flown talk about patriotism was not often heard. Instead people wondered what the world would be like afterward. How could they prevent another world war?

As the war started, Minnesota was labeled an isolationist state. Most of its congressmen and senators had leaned toward neutrality. Many Minnesotans hung back from close ties to other countries. But the state's young governor, Harold Stassen, believed the United States should be more active in world affairs. He supported Wendell Willkie, who ran for president in 1940. Later Willkie wrote a book called *One World*. He argued that industry and transportation were making the world too small a place for each nation to go its own way.

Minneapolis buildings that rose in the 1970s and 1980s have dwarfed the Foshay Tower. Below them traffic flows along Interstate 94. In the years after World War II such highways sliced wide canyons through the neighborhoods of Minneapolis and other cities.

By the end of the war it was clear, in Stassen's words, "that the walls of isolation are gone forever." When the Senate voted in 1945 to join the United Nations, only two senators opposed it. Minnesota's Henrik Shipstead was one. Shipstead had been popular with state voters for 23 years. But their views were changing. In the 1946 election he lost by a landslide.

The next 40 years saw Minnesota drawn steadily closer to the rest of the world. Boundaries of all kinds faded. Not only did the old lines between regions, countries, and people seem less important. Finding clear lines between industries and ideas and ways of doing things was harder.

Farms and Industry

Among boundaries that nearly disappeared was the one between farming and industry. After World War II industrialism finally turned farms into factories. Between 1945 and 1985 American agriculture changed more than ever before. The cluster of jobs that had always made up life on a farm became separate businesses.

Raising chickens was one example. On almost every older farm, hens pecked at bugs in barnyards and laid eggs in nests. Now a chicken is seldom seen scratching in the dirt. They live in big buildings with thousands of others. Hens spend their whole lives in cages. Automatic equipment gives them just the right amounts of food, water, heat, light, and medicines to make them grow fast. Machines collect and sort the eggs.

Harold E. Stassen was a brilliant young man. At 31, he was the youngest governor ever elected in the country. His leadership gave new life to Minnesota's Republican party. Voters reelected him twice.

During World War II Stassen left the Minnesota governor's office to join the navy. Already his interest in world affairs was well known. So President Roosevelt chose him in 1945 to help write the charter for the United Nations.

In those years many people thought Harold Stassen would be president some day. So did he. But luck and politics seemed against him. He served as a top advisor to President Dwight Eisenhower in the 1950s. Until 1955 he was in charge of the U.S. foreign aid program that helped put Europe back on its feet after World War II. Later he became an assistant on questions of disarmament. In that position some called him the president's "Secretary of Peace."

It takes a lot of money to start such a business, but scientific control gets much more from the chickens. Today's specially bred "superchicken" produces twice as many eggs as a barnyard hen did. The birds are not as strong or healthy, but the cost of eggs is less. Some people wonder whether this is fair to the chickens. Others ask whether the manager of such a business can be called a farmer.

Much the same kind of thing has happened to hogs and cattle. They are fattened in automated feedlots. And most farm families no longer keep a few cows. Now dairy farms produce nearly all the milk sold. In large barns whole herds of cows are fed and milked by machines. These animals, too, are bred to give the kinds of meat or milk people want to buy. As the 1990s approached, there was talk of making "supercows" through genetic engineering. They would produce twice as much milk as normal animals.

Scientists also have bred new kinds of plants. These produce more kernels of corn and more grains of wheat. Some resist plant diseases like wheat rust. So harvests from the same fields are greater than ever before. Chemists have created new products to kill insects and weeds. They have also made stronger fertilizers. All these developments are sometimes called "the green revolution."

In 1940 half the state's farmers still did not own tractors. By the 1980s you could not farm without one—or several. Modern tractors are heavier and more powerful. They have enclosed cabs instead of open seats. Some have air-conditioning, stereo, and two-way radios. With these huge

Norman E. Borlaug is a scientist who played a key part in bringing about the green revolution all over the world. He was the son of Norwegian-American farmers in northeastern Iowa. At the University of Minnesota he studied the diseases of plants.

During the 1940s and 1950s Borlaug tackled the wheat rust that ruined crops in Mexico. After years of work, he bred a kind of wheat that did not get rust. The sturdy plant had many more grains than older kinds. At last Mexican farmers were able to grow enough wheat for their country.

In the 1960s Borlaug went to India and Pakistan. He showed them new ways to feed their starving people. In 1970 he received the Nobel Peace Prize for his fight against world hunger. Poverty and misery wipe out boundaries, Borlaug said. He warned nations not to "dream of isolation" while there was hunger anywhere.

Cows disappear behind machines at this modern "milking parlor" in Stearns County.

tractors, a farmer can plow or harvest many rows at once. Other kinds of machinery have also been added. On some farms irrigation rigs roll across whole fields, watering crops at just the right time.

These changes have helped Minnesota farms set new production records year after year. At the same time fewer workers have been needed. From 1940 to 1980 more than half the state's farmers left their land. By the mid-1980s only about 5 percent of Minnesotans lived and worked on farms. The changes came from the pressure to produce more food for less money. Successful farmers could not afford to count the costs paid by soil, animals, and people.

Country and City

During earlier times cities reached out to the country in many ways. After World War II the boundary between country and city began to disappear. It was crossed by wider and faster highways. It was blurred by people going many miles to jobs and schools and stores. It was erased by new telephone and electric power lines.

In 1940 just over a quarter of Minnesota farm homes had electricity. By 1959 nearly all had it. Soon they also had refrigerators, freezers, washers, dryers, television sets, and air-conditioners. Farmhouses began to look much like homes in cities and suburbs. Jobs like canning and butchering were done in towns. Farmers, like city people, drove to the supermarket for food. Some farmers even lived in towns and drove to their fields for work.

Steiger tractors are often seen in the Red River Valley. The company that builds them started in Red Lake Falls and later moved to Fargo, North Dakota.

Minnesota industries also helped to rub out the boundary between city and country. In the 1980s more Minnesotans than ever worked in mills and factories. But no longer were they all in cities. Duluth's steel mill closed in the 1970s. At the same time taconite plants were opening in the woods of northeastern Minnesota. Workers drove many miles or moved to new "taconite towns" like Silver Bay and Hoyt Lakes. Also in the 1970s the huge stockyards of South St. Paul closed down. Meat-packing shifted to smaller plants nearer to where cattle were raised.

Before World War II the word *electronics* was almost unknown. By the 1970s more than 70,000 Minnesotans did work related to it. They made computers, medical and scientific equipment, aircraft and missile parts, and other things that called for training and skill. Some of the new "high-tech" industries stayed in the cities. Many moved to suburbs. Others built plants in smaller towns.

As suburbs spread through seven counties around the Twin Cities, they outgrew old boundaries. The dozens of town and city governments already there did not always work smoothly together. In 1957 the state created a planning commission for the whole area. Ten years later it was given new power as the Metropolitan Council.

Still more was happening. As freeways reached out, homes and businesses followed. People who worked at plants or shopping malls in the suburbs often lived far out in the country. Summer cabins became year-round homes. Country towns that had served farmers for a hundred years became "bedroom communities" for cities.

Snowmobiles like this early model were invented after World War II. They became an important industry in northern Minnesota.

Many of the people from these suburban homes in Hawley drive to jobs in Moorhead and Fargo.

In the mid-1980s geographers saw an "urban corridor" running from Rochester through the Twin Cities to St. Cloud. They predicted that 60 percent of the state's people would soon live there. Others foresaw an even larger, semi-urban triangle with points at Two Harbors, La Crosse, Wisconsin, and Fargo-Moorhead. Throughout this triangle, they claimed, population was steadily growing. Some day most of it would be neither real city nor true countryside.

Ties to the World

Freeways do not end at state borders. By the end of the 1970s you could drive from the Twin Cities to New York without passing a stoplight. But this was only one way that new transportation brought Minnesota nearer to the rest of the world.

After World War II, industry and agriculture grew fat on cheap energy. Both needed more oil and natural gas than ever before. Minnesota has neither. Gas could only be brought by pipes. Oil, too, was cheaper that way. In the 1950s pipelines linked Minnesota to Texas and Oklahoma. Later, lines reached across the plains from oil and gas fields in North Dakota and Canada.

In the 1850s Minnesotans had dreamed of ocean ships sailing through the Great Lakes. A hundred years later, the dream came true. In 1959 the St. Lawrence Seaway was finished. Duluth became a world port. Since then foreign ships have been common in its harbor. Most often they are seen loading wheat from the Great Plains.

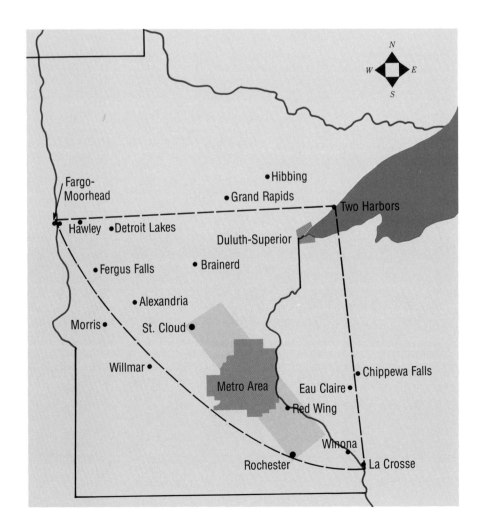

Forecasters of the 1980s predicted the growth of an urban band (light shaded area) through the Twin Cities from southeast to northwest. They expected population growth in central and southeastern Minnesota and northwestern Wisconsin as shown by the broken line.

Meanwhile work begun on the upper Mississippi in the 1930s was being finished. Twenty-seven dams turned the river into a chain of ponds. They climb like steps from St. Louis to Minneapolis. Locks at each dam raise or lower boats and barges to the next level. The last set of locks was done in 1963.

Waterways and pipelines carry fuel and heavy freight. People travel by air. Northwest Orient (now Northwest) is Minnesota's largest airline. It started in 1926. Until World War II air travel was an exciting luxury. After the war it became common. By 1980 Twin Cities International Airport was one spot on a worldwide network of airways. Direct flights brought Minnesota within a few hours of Europe and Asia.

In the 1980s Minnesota's metropolitan area was no longer on the fringe of things. It was known nationwide for music, drama, and art. The Tyrone Guthrie Theater opened and big league sports came in the 1960s. The University of Minnesota hospitals and the Mayo Clinic made Minnesota a world medical center. Tourists, health-seekers, and business people from many countries visited the state.

Among the faces from different lands were also new immigrants. In the years after World War II refugees from many places reached Minnesota. There were Lithuanians, Latvians, Hungarians, Cubans, and in the 1980s thousands of people from Southeast Asia. Immigrants also arrived from Mexico and Central America. Many of these came by way of states in the Southwest. In 1975 Latin-Americans were Minnesota's largest minority group.

St. Paul's World Trade Center, built in the 1980s, serves the growing number of Minnesota companies with international ties.

Loading grain onto a ship in the Duluth harbor

A Role in World Affairs

Minnesota has a new place on the national as well as on the world map. Since the end of World War II, state leaders have played an important part in the U.S. government and its foreign policy. In turn, world events have shaped Minnesota politics more than ever before.

In 1943 Minnesota's Farmer-Labor party joined with the Democrats to form the Democratic-Farmer-Labor party, or DFL. Five years later, the new DFL split over U.S. policy toward the Soviet Union. One group, led by former governor Elmer Benson, favored cooperation with communist countries. A stronger group was headed by Hubert Humphrey, the young mayor of Minneapolis. He supported the "cold war" on communism. After a bitter struggle, the Benson group left the party. Humphrey was elected U.S. senator from Minnesota in 1948. He held that office and led the DFL party until 1964. Then he became vice-president of the United States.

Through the 1950s Hubert Humphrey, like his fellow Minnesotan, Harold Stassen, was a strong voice in U.S. foreign policy. The two belonged to different parties, but their views were much alike. Both men were friends of the United Nations. They believed that economic aid to poor countries was a better weapon against communism than threats of war. They worked to stop testing of nuclear arms.

In the 1960s the United States entered the Vietnam war. As vice-president, Humphrey supported this. But many Americans opposed it. There were peace marches and public protests. Young men fled to Canada to avoid being drafted. Then the nation heard another Minnesota voice. In

Walter H. Judd was a medical missionary in China during the 1930s, when Japanese troops invaded. Back in this country, he urged that the United States stop all trade with Japan. By 1941 Judd was a doctor in Minneapolis, but he still gave speeches on the Far East. When Japan attacked the United States that year, his friends said he had been right. They urged him to run for Congress. Because he felt so strongly about questions of foreign policy, he did.

Congressman Judd was one of the leaders who drew Minnesota away from isolationism. Like Stassen, he believed in the United Nations. He felt, however, that communist countries should be kept out of world government. For years he spoke fiercely against any U.S. relations with the People's Republic of China.

Eugenie Moore Anderson of Red Wing was one of the young, forceful leaders who helped create Minnesota's DFL party in 1944. Four years later she held an office in the national Democratic party. When the DFL split in 1948, she backed Hubert Humphrey.

In 1949 President Harry Truman made her the first American woman ambassador. She went to Denmark. Her appointment was a tribute to women in the Democratic party. It also repaid Minnesota's support for a tough U.S. policy in world affairs. From 1962 to 1964 President John Kennedy sent Eugenie Anderson to Bulgaria. So she also became the first woman to represent the United States in a country allied with the Soviet Union.

1967 Senator Eugene McCarthy spoke out for the antiwar groups. Next year the Democratic party had to choose which of the two Minnesotans it wanted to run for president. Protesters in the streets shouted for McCarthy. Delegates in the convention hall chose Humphrey. Later the country's voters elected Republican Richard M. Nixon.

Through the 1970s and into the 1980s Minnesotans kept on being heard in national and world affairs. Warren Burger of St. Paul became chief justice of the U.S. Supreme Court. Another Minnesotan on the nation's highest court was Justice Harry Blackmun. Several men from the state served as cabinet officers. And soon Minnesota again had a U.S. vice-president. In 1976 Walter Mondale was elected along with Democratic President Jimmy Carter. In 1984 Mondale ran for president. Like Humphrey, he was defeated.

Minnesotans protesting against the Vietnam war

Hubert H. Humphrey was "the man from Minnesota" in the 30 years following World War II. People all over the world who had never heard or thought about the state learned of it because of him. Many Minnesotans disagreed with him. Yet most of them liked him. It was hard not to. He argued endlessly for what he believed in. But he did so without anger, even when he was beaten.

One of the things Humphrey believed in most was civil rights for blacks and other minority peoples. While he was mayor, Minneapolis adopted the nation's first fair employment law. He gave a famous speech for civil rights at the Democratic national convention in 1948. In foreign affairs he is remembered for a daylong talk with Soviet premier Nikita Khrushchev (Ni-KEE-ta KROOS-chahv) in 1958. The two men discussed world problems and ways to avoid war. Humphrey is also remembered as the sponsor of programs like Food for Peace and the Peace Corps.

Humphrey wanted very much to be president and tried several times for the office. After Nixon narrowly defeated him in 1968, Humphrey returned to Minnesota. In 1971 the state's voters sent him again to the U.S. Senate. He served there until his death in 1978.

Chapter 20
Trends and Problems

How Long Is a Lifetime?

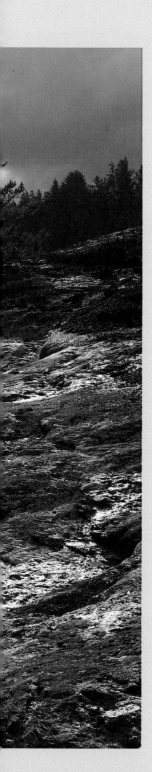

R hoda Kimbro was born in 1896 on a farm near Canby, Minnesota. In 1986 she was 90 years old. The ways of living and thinking she knew as a child were closer to people a thousand years earlier than to the world of 1986.

The changes Rhoda has seen are not just electric lights, telephones, stereos, television, air-conditioners, microwave ovens, computers, and the other gadgets that have transformed daily life. Important as those are, they are only part of the story. Another is the number of people alive. In 90 years the earth has grown a lot more crowded. There were one-and-a-half billion humans in 1900. In 1986 there were nearly five billion. Minnesota's population grew from one-and-three-quarters million to over four million. More people live in the state today than the total of all who have lived here in the past.

When Rhoda was a child, people still thought of the natural world as something that would always limit human power. Ninety years later, science had given humans the means to destroy both themselves and nature. Nuclear weapons threatened the existence of all living things.

Rhoda was born at home. A neighbor woman helped her mother. No doctor came. When Rhoda's little sister was dying of infant cholera, their mother nursed the sick child herself. Few people went to hospitals. Later another sister got scarlet fever, and Rhoda stayed with friends to keep from catching it. By the 1980s drugs had made those diseases and many others almost unknown in Minnesota. Still, there were more and larger hospitals than ever before. Most people were born in one, went there if they were sick, and died there when the time came.

Birth, death, and illness were all parts of family life when Rhoda was a child. Most aged, disabled, and mentally ill people lived with their relatives and were cared for by them. Small children, too, were looked after by families, as they always had been. There were no nursery schools or day-care centers, or even kindergartens. Welfare programs, social workers, and therapists did not exist. Now many families can no longer give these kinds of care. They have become jobs for someone else.

The uncrowded beauty of Minnesota's northern border country appears in this photo of Rainy Lake. Part of it has been preserved as roadless wilderness in the Boundary Waters Canoe Area. Some is in Voyageurs National Park. There is disagreement over using or protecting the land.

When Rhoda was two years old, her family moved. They loaded everything into a wagon, just as her great-grandparents and their great-grandparents had done. It took two weeks to travel from Yellow Medicine County in Minnesota to central Iowa. Rhoda was 14 before she rode in a car and 19 when she first saw an airplane. In her thirties she learned to drive, and in her sixties she flew across the ocean in a day. Twenty years later, when she was in her eighties, she dialed a number on her phone in St. Paul and talked by satellite to her daughter in Italy. In the meantime she had watched on television as people traveled in rockets to the moon.

The greatest changes Rhoda can remember came after World War II. In ancient times a small change might have taken hundreds of years. Now small changes happen in a few months. Each new idea or way of doing things brings the next one faster. This speeding up has created problems as well as achievements. Great changes often bring unexpected results.

Change at the Roots

Science and industry brought more material goods and comfort than anyone dreamed of at the beginning of the 20th century. But even then, some people felt uneasy. They had good reason. In changing how everyone works and depends on others, the new system reached to the very roots of life.

Communities now care for people in many ways that families used to—for example in hospitals and daycare centers. So families have less power over their members than they once did, and communities have

Rhoda Kimbro, the author's mother, is shown above at age 14. The picture at right was taken when she was 84.

more. Today most of us think that an individual has rights from the moment he or she is born—or even earlier. Communities feel they must protect the human rights of all persons, sometimes against the claims of their own family. This was not always so.

Some of the hardest problems people face at the end of the 20th century are presented by changing patterns of family life. In the last 25 years Minnesotans, like others, have struggled and argued over questions like no-fault divorce, child abuse, abortion, and gay rights. In addition, science now gives people greater power over life and death. This brings up still more disturbing issues.

Related to our changing view of the rights of individuals is the question of equal treatment for women. As soon as their long fight for suffrage was won in the early 1920s, some women began working for the next step. They wanted an amendment to the U.S. Constitution that would make them equal in all laws. Not everyone agreed. Some felt that special laws were needed to protect women. They feared an equal rights amendment would block such protection.

Forty years went by without much change. But during World War II the country urged women to help by replacing men who had gone into the armed forces. Thousands worked in offices, factories, and mines. Many kept on after the war ended. In the years since then, more than half of America's women have turned from being full-time homemakers to being workers with jobs. But most of them have never earned as much money as

The Ramsey County Medical Center is like many hospital complexes throughout the country. It shows how much people have grown to depend on community medical and social services.

men. In the 1960s the anger of women began to build. Minority groups were demanding equal treatment in education, jobs, and other areas. In the 1970s women joined the movement.

Congress passed an equal rights amendment and sent it to the states for their agreement. Minnesota, along with 34 other states, ratified the amendment. But three more states were needed, and it was not adopted.

Laws were not the whole story. Women worked for equality in many other ways. In Minnesota, groups like the Women's Political Caucus helped women run for office and urged others to vote for them. Through the 1950s only one woman served in the Minnesota legislature. The number grew steadily after that, and by 1988 there were 31. In that year women also held two other state offices. Joan Growe was secretary of state, and Marlene Johnson was the first woman to serve as lieutenant governor. Rosalie Wahl had become the first woman judge on the Minnesota Supreme Court in 1977.

In December 1977, eight women who worked for a bank in Willmar went on strike. They said the bank was unfair. Four of its five officers were men. All of its 12 lower-paid clerks were women. When the bank hired a new officer, it did not let the women apply for the job. Instead it hired a man without experience and told some of the women to train him. When they asked the bank's president about this, he answered: "We're not all equal, you know."

For Jeannette Ridlon Piccard equality for women went deeper than law, politics, or pay. At the age of 79 she became what she had always wanted to be—an Episcopal priest.

When she was young her wish seemed impossible. Women could not be priests. She went to college and graduate school and then married Jean (Zhon) Felix Piccard. He was a Swiss scientist interested in the upper atmosphere. In 1934, long before the time of rockets or satellites, the Piccards rode a balloon to a record height. Jeannette piloted the craft while Jean took readings.

A short time later the Piccards moved to Minnesota. Jean taught at the university. In the 1960s Jeannette lectured around the country for the National Aeronautics and Space Administration (NASA). In her travels she also talked with Episcopal church people about priesthood for women. Slowly change came. In 1974 she and ten other women were ordained against church rules. They were legally accepted as priests in 1977.

Women worked side by side with men in Twin Cities factories during World War II.

The Willmar strike drew attention all over the country. Many women worked in banks without hope of being promoted. Yet it was the first such strike anyone could remember. The women stuck to it for two years. Some of their neighbors made fun of them. They got little support from labor unions and none from the government or the law. The bank refused to hire them back.

For the "Willmar Eight" it was a sad defeat. Their lives would never be quite the same again. But in a way they also won. Newspapers, television, and women's groups spread their story. Two films were made about them. Meanwhile, across Minnesota and elsewhere, banks quietly began to make some changes. Glennis Ter Wisscha, the youngest of the eight, said later: "There have always been people who have fought hard and long, given up their personal life, given up their own goals, for a cause."

Minorities on the Move

Like women, blacks and Indians found that service in the armed forces and wartime jobs opened new doors. Thousands moved to cities during World War II. After the war ended, both groups faced pressures that kept them there.

Many black people had worked on farms in the South. The new machines and other changes in farming took away their jobs. So the stream of blacks moving north to big cities in search of work kept on through the 1950s and 1960s. In Minnesota the number grew from 14,000 in 1950 to 52,000 in 1980. Most of them live in the metropolitan area, as Minnesota

In winter as well as summer, members of the Willmar Eight picketed the Citizens National Bank.

blacks always have. Like black communities elsewhere in the country, they have struggled for equal treatment in jobs, in schools, and in housing.

During the same years the United States had a policy of relocating Indian people. The government sent them to cities where they could find jobs. It hoped in this way to make them "independent." Many Indians suspected this was a new way of saying they should give up their rights and traditions. Some had to move. But ties to family and friends and to their land often drew them home again.

Like other minorities, Indians demanded jobs and equal treatment. But they also wanted land and treaty rights that had been taken from them. Such things, some insisted, could not be paid for by money. The land was sacred, they said. Without it, Indians could not exist as a separate people.

These were disturbing thoughts to most other Americans. Like their ancestors, whites thought of land as something to buy and sell. If it were fertile, it should be farmed. If it held minerals, it should be mined. They were disturbed, too, to find that many Indian people still wanted to keep their beliefs and live in their own communities under their own rules.

Local People Speak Up

Other people, too, wanted more to say about things that affected their lives. As corporations and governments grew bigger, those who lived in city neighborhoods and small towns began to feel powerless. They joined together to block decisions they thought were unjust. Sometimes they sued in court. Sometimes

August Wilson moved to Minnesota in the 1970s. He was trying to get started as a writer. Like others, he found the Twin Cities a good place for working in the arts. Soon his plays about the lives of black people began to draw attention. In 1987 one called *Fences* became a Broadway hit and won three national prizes. Wilson stayed on in St. Paul. The Minnesota black community still welcomes and supports new talent, just as it did with John Q. Adams a hundred years ago.

they protested in public. In western Minnesota during the 1970s a group of farmers went even further.

The dispute was over a power line. Everyone was talking about energy. There was an oil shortage, and the country was looking for ways to make more use of its coal. Minnesota is an energy-poor state. It has no oil, gas, or coal, and not much waterpower. But North Dakota has great beds of low-grade coal, called lignite. This coal was not being used because it cost too much to ship. A lot was needed to produce a little energy. In 1973 some Minnesota electric companies suggested building a power plant near the lignite and moving the electricity instead. They would build a huge long-distance line, reaching from central North Dakota to the Twin Cities.

The plan was already set when the companies began to tell farmers in western Minnesota about the line crossing their land. There was a storm of anger. No one wanted the ugly towers. They feared the new kind of high-tension line would hurt the health of people and animals. They felt their land was being harmed so city people could use more power. They argued for saving energy and getting it from sources like the sun and windmills instead of coal.

Local officials refused to let the line go through. Then the companies turned to the state. Hearings were held, and farmers spoke. Later they protested at the Capitol. Grant County farmer Jim Nelson was one. He believed that "People felt none of what they said was really heard. The state never seriously considered whether the line was needed. The decision had been made before the hearings began."

Russell Means (left) and Dennis Banks, two leaders of AIM

In St. Paul's Red School House Indian people teach their children traditional ways along with other subjects.

The American Indian Movement—usually called AIM—started in Minneapolis in 1968. Its leaders were young and poor. Some had been in prison. They wanted to return to more traditional Indian ways. They also demanded land and other rights that had been promised to their tribes in treaties.

In 1972 AIM called for a march to Washington along "the Trail of Broken Treaties." The marchers started peacefully. They ended by camping in the offices of the Bureau of Indian Affairs and fighting police. In the spring of 1973 followers of AIM took over the small Indian community of Wounded Knee, South Dakota, as a protest. They claimed that the elected tribal government of the Pine Ridge Reservation was corrupt. They said it was giving up Indian land rights to white businesses. Federal and tribal police surrounded the village. There were threats and gunfire. The siege of Wounded Knee lasted 71 days, and several people were killed. AIM leaders were later tried in a St. Paul court and acquitted of wrongdoing.

The farmers were not ready to give up. When company workers went out to build the line, people blocked the roads. Hundreds of police were sent. Many men and women were arrested as they tried to keep the crews off their land. After the line was finally built, the big steel towers began to fall. Someone kept loosening the bolts that held them up. But as years went by, the fight slowly ended. Those who wanted more power in cities and suburbs had won.

Progress and Pollution

Energy was only one part of a many-sided problem that began to worry people deeply in the 1970s and 1980s. There were signs that industrialism in cities and on farms was harming the environment—the land, the air, and the water. The problem was worldwide, but Minnesotans talked about it more than some others. The state has always been proud of its fertile fields, its forests, and its thousands of clear lakes.

Protecting the environment often means hard choices. Minnesota has had its share of these. One of them led to the longest court case ever fought over pollution.

In the early 1950s, as Minnesota's rich ore was running out, everyone hoped the steel companies could use taconite. Jobs for thousands of people depended on it. But it had not really been tried. Reserve Mining Company took a risk and led the way. In 1951 it started to build the first large taconite plant. It chose a location at Silver Bay, on the shore of Lake Superior.

The route of the power line from North Dakota to the metropolitan area (shaded). Most protests were in Grant, Pope, and Stearns counties.

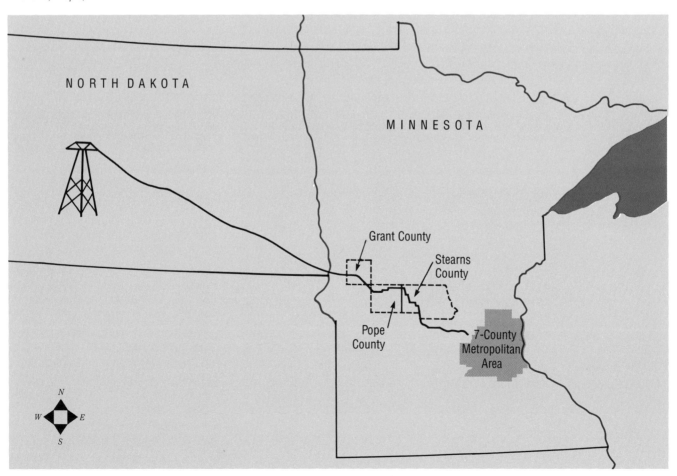

One problem in processing taconite is getting rid of tons of powdered rock after the iron has been taken out. This finely crushed rock is called tailings. Reserve solved the problem by dumping the tailings into the lake. A few people objected. Superior is the largest and deepest freshwater lake in the world. Many communities use its clear, pure water for drinking. Its beautiful, unspoiled north shore brings thousands of tourists to Minnesota. But people were eager for the new taconite plant to succeed. Tests seemed to show that the tailings would sink to the bottom without harming the lake. So the dumping was allowed.

Over the next 18 years many things changed. Taconite became an important industry. Reserve tripled the size of its plant. A new town grew up around it. But the lake in front of the plant was filled with ugly banks of black mud. Patches of cloudy green water were seen for many miles along the shore. Fishermen claimed that fish were dying. Many people began to call for an end to the pollution.

In 1968 a U.S. government study raised serious questions about what the dumping was doing to Lake Superior. The company replied that the study was full of errors. After four years of argument, the federal government sued.

By then scientists knew that taconite tailings were not all at the bottom of the lake. People in towns like Two Harbors and Duluth were drinking them in the water from their faucets. But everyone thought they were harmless. Early in the 1970s it was learned that food with asbestos fibers

Gloria Woida and her husband, Math, owned a farm in Stearns County. Math had worked on the land with his father from the time he was 15. He and Gloria had raised four children there. In 1976 they learned the power line would run through their land.

"I used to sit home," Gloria remembered, "and be a real quiet mama and take care of the kids and work on the farm. But all of a sudden the power line comes around one day, and it opens up your eyes to what people really have to do. I will never shut up and be quiet again."

She went to meetings with Math and began to speak out. People listened. The meetings ended and the power company crews finally came. Farmers stood facing a line of state troopers in their own fields. By then women like Gloria were among the leaders of the protest. She was arrested. It was hard—"almost a little bit like dying." But "I wish, looking back, I'd have sat down every day and been hauled off. That's the best way to protest and make a difference."

Power-line protesters in Stearns County

Judge Miles Lord

in it causes cancer. In 1974 someone pointed out that the taconite mined by Reserve has fibers much like asbestos. Federal and state agencies did more testing, then put out a warning. Alarm spread. People began to drink bottled water. Duluth and other towns looked for ways to filter out the dangerous fibers.

The government's case against Reserve Mining had been in court for nearly two years. By April 1974, the threat to public health was clear. Judge Miles Lord ordered the company to stop dumping tailings into the lake at once. Next day the plant was closed. More than three thousand people suddenly found themselves out of work. Reserve appealed to a higher court. There Judge Lord's order was reversed, and the plant reopened.

A new way to get rid of the taconite tailings had to be found. But six more years of court hearings went by before the state and the company could agree on a place to put them. At last, in April 1980, Reserve stopped dumping them into Lake Superior.

As the 1980s went on, people learned of greater dangers to the environment and even harder choices to be made. Chemicals in the fertilizers, insect sprays, and weed killers that allow farmers to grow large crops were sinking through the soil. Slowly they poisoned the water deep in the rocks below. Country people and many towns depended on this "ground water" for pure wells.

Tailings spread into Lake Superior from the plant at Silver Bay.

Gases from millions of car engines and from coal-burning power plants were gathering in the clouds and producing "acid rain." In Minnesota's north country and across the border in Canada, it killed fish in the clear, rocky lakes and turned forests brown with dying trees. The question of where to put dangerous chemicals and waste materials had become a nightmare. Many already dumped in out-of-the-way places had to be cleaned up. More were collecting. Even more dangerous were radioactive materials from nuclear reactors. No one yet knew a really safe place to store them.

All of these problems are larger than one state. But facing them makes people look again at the land called Minnesota. Settlers from Europe took it, thinking they could make better use of it than Indian people. In less than 150 years they changed it more than it had changed in nearly 10,000 years before. Their dreams and hard work and the richness of the land improved life for millions of people. But some wonder about the cost. What kind of place will the country of sky-colored waters be after another 150 years? Will it turn into a wasteland? Or will our children and grandchildren learn to live in a way that does not destroy it?

Split Rock Lighthouse was built to warn ships away from the cliffs. Now it is a beacon to tourists. Only a few miles from Silver Bay, it stands in one of ten state parks along Minnesota's North Shore.

Chapter 21
The Idea of Minnesota

Many Minnesotas

What is a state? We all know the shape on the map, the license plates, and the highway signs at the border. We know about the state capital, the state constitution, and the laws that govern much of our lives. But the real state is the land and the people who live on it. It is also the idea or image we have that makes it different from other places.

To see an image of yourself, you look in a mirror. The mirror for a place is the stories, songs, and pictures of it. Sometimes it is in symbols adopted by its people or in jokes they tell about it. These things may be what we call folklore—traditions that grow and spread among a group of people, changing as they pass around. Or they may be art and literature composed by a known person. Often they are a trademark designed to sell or promote.

Minnesota is a place of many faces. It also has had many images. They have been different on the Iron Range, in the north woods, beside the Red River, or on the streets of St. Paul and Minneapolis. Each region has had traditions and an image of its own.

Some regions reach beyond Minnesota. One that crosses the boundaries of states and countries is the Red River Valley. When the Red River floods (as it often does), it spreads over parts of North Dakota and Manitoba as well as Minnesota. The borders that separate governments mean nothing to the water. Memories and traditions have spread in much the same way. One such tradition is a sad tune called "The Red River Valley."

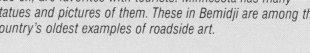

The mythical lumberjack, Paul Bunyan, and Babe, his big blue ox, are favorites with tourists. Minnesota has many statues and pictures of them. These in Bemidji are among the country's oldest examples of roadside art.

Some say it was sung around campfires on the oxcart trails to St. Paul. The earliest words tell of a heartbroken métis woman and a blue-eyed trader or soldier. He is returning to his "home by the ocean" and leaving her behind. The song was remembered for years in Canada, then it came to the United States. There people gave it new words. In the South, ranchers adopted it for the Red River between Texas and Oklahoma. Instead of "the grief of the Red River girl," they sang about "the cowboy who loves you so true." In that form it became popular all over the West. But the lonesome-sounding tune belonged first to the land of the métis.

On the Iron Range, too, there was an image of loneliness. Along with it people saw strength and independence. There they told stories about Otto Walta, who had come from Finland to be a miner. Disgusted with working for others, Otto took a homestead deep in the woods. He lived there for many years alone.

Once he borrowed an iron rail from a train track to use in prying tree stumps out of the ground. Otto was so strong he carried it three miles to his farm. After a while the railroad company sent some men to claim it. He said sure, they could take it. But they didn't bother. A whole crew would have been needed to get it back to the track.

Otto was also soft-hearted. He wouldn't kill a bedbug or a flea. Instead, he just moved to a new bed. And he wouldn't make his poor old horse pull a plow through the roots and stones in his field. He pushed the plow by himself.

This young Minnesota woman, probably métis, was drawn in the 1850s.

One early Canadian version of "The Red River Valley" has these verses:

From this valley they say you are going,
I shall miss your blue eyes and sweet smile,
And you take with you all of the sunshine
That has brightened my pathway a while.

As you go to your home by the ocean
May you never forget those sweet hours
That we spent in the Red River Valley
And the love we exchanged 'mid its bowers.

There never could be such a longing
In the heart of a pale maiden's breast
As dwells in the heart you are breaking
With love for the boy who came west.

And the dark maiden's prayer for her lover
To the Spirit that rules all this world
Is that sunshine his pathway may cover
And the grief of the Red River Girl.

Chorus:
So consider a while ere you leave me
Do not hasten to bid me adieu,
But remember the Red River Valley
And the half-breed that loved you so true.

In the Twin Cities Swedish immigrants had stories about tall, blond Ola Värmlänning (Oo-la Vairm-len-ing). He was, some said, the wandering son of a well-to-do family in the part of Sweden called Värmland. Unlike Otto Walta, the backwoods loner, Ola loved practical jokes. There was the time he met a crowd of new Swedish immigrants in St. Paul. They did not speak English. He pretended to be a city official and told them they could all have jobs. They were to dig up the pavement on Seventh Street. It was nearly done before the police could stop them.

Yankee lumberjacks had their own hero. Like the Red River song, he belonged to more than Minnesota. In forests from Maine to the Pacific Coast they told stories of Paul Bunyan. Many were about how Paul solved problems. Like the time there was a log jam 200 feet high and a mile long. Paul led Babe, his big blue ox, into the river ahead of the jam. Then he stood on the bank and shot at Babe with a rifle. The ox thought the bullets were flies biting. It started twisting its tail to drive them off. The whirling tail acted like a big propeller and drove the river right back upstream. When the water rose, the logs floated free.

The Mirror Gets Polished

Otto Walta and Ola Värmlänning stayed close to their own places and their own people. Paul Bunyan was different. In 1914 the Red River Lumber Company of Minneapolis printed a pamphlet with stories about him. Paul's fame spread. Writers everywhere claimed him. They made up new stories and changed him from a clever Yankee lumberjack to a frontier giant. The blue ox grew, too. It took a

Many Swedish immigrants lived at first in "Swede Hollow" on St. Paul's East Side. It is shown here in an etching by George Resler.

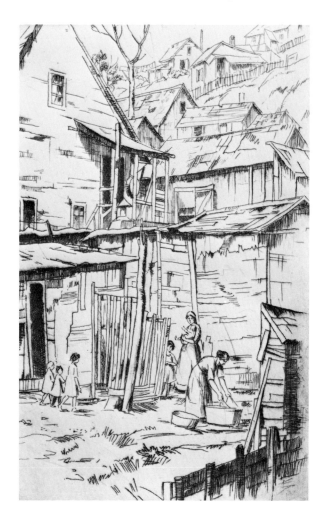

whole iron mine to make shoes for Babe. So he could lie down, they logged off North Dakota. That is why there are no trees there. He pulled the kinks out of crooked logging roads. And he hauled whole sections of land to the river so they could cut the trees right into the stream. When a tank of water Babe was hauling broke open, it made the Mississippi River.

The new Paul Bunyan not only mowed down forests. He grew sky-high corn in Kansas, dug oil wells in Texas, and rearranged lakes, rivers, and mountains. Once he built a hotel so tall the top stories had to swing away to let the moon go by. He became a symbol for all America. Bigger was better. And overnight, it seemed, he could remake the land to suit himself.

Paul Bunyan was not the only image changed and polished by writers. Another was Winabojo (Win-uh-bo-ZHO), a hero of the Ojibway Indians. Their stories tell how Winabojo played tricks, and also how he helped both animals and humans. In the mid-1800s a popular poet, Henry W. Longfellow, wrote a long story-poem called *The Song of Hiawatha.* In it he mixed up tales from different Indian groups around the country. The name Hiawatha came from an eastern tribe, but many of the adventures belonged to Winabojo. Longfellow had also read Mary Eastman's book about the Dakota and had seen a picture of the lovely waterfall near Fort Snelling. He was told that the Dakota called it "Minnehaha," or Laughing Water. He gave that name to the Indian maiden Hiawatha loved.

A statue of Hiawatha and Minnehaha was placed in Minnehaha Park just above the falls in 1911. Minnesota school children paid for it by giving more than $1,000 in pennies. Sculptor Jacob Fjelde (FYELL-duh) got the idea from Longfellow's lines:

Over wide and rushing rivers
In his arms he bore the maiden;
Light he thought her as a feather,
As the plume upon his head-gear.

Minnehaha Falls about 1907

Longfellow's poem had little to do with real Indian traditions, but white people liked the romantic story. It brought hundreds of visitors to Minneapolis each year to see

Where the Falls of Minnehaha
Flash and gleam among the oak-trees,
Laugh and leap into the valley.

Postcards and calendars by the thousands showed the noble Hiawatha carrying Minnehaha across the stream. For many years the state promoted this made-up Indian image. In the 1970s the department of tourism still advertised southern Minnesota as "Hiawathaland."

Symbols are sometimes chosen to promote a place—and sometimes not. In 1858 railroad builders were trying to get the state government to lend them money for laying tracks. A popular cartoon showed the railroad men as gophers in top hats. The idea tickled the humor of Minnesota farm people. To them gophers were number-one pests. But the railroad got the money—and farmers started calling Minnesota the Gopher State. The name stuck. As years passed most people forgot how it had started. But Minnesota was still farmers' country. The busy little gopher or ground squirrel, digging holes and poking its head up in fields and pastures, seemed a fitting symbol.

The 1980s were different. Everywhere were pictures of the state bird—the loon. It reminded people of lakes and wildlife and quiet wilder-

Loons on a northern lake

ness—the kind of things that now bring thousands of tourists. Most Minnesotans, too, liked to think of their state in that way. More than half of them lived in cities. They treasured the idea of unspoiled nature somewhere "up north"—and not so very far away.

The Small-Town Image

City dwellers who like the idea of wilderness are less certain about small towns. Yet more than either farms or wilderness, small towns have been one of the lasting images of Minnesota. During the 1850s, when people were trying to get rich quick by laying out new towns and selling land, a Minnesota minister named Edward Eggleston wrote a popular book. In it he poked fun at the boosters of Metropolisville, a small town with big hopes somewhere in southeastern Minnesota. Eggleston's book is seldom heard of now, but Metropolisville was followed by other more famous towns. Like it, they cannot be found on any map.

In 1920 a young Minnesotan named Sinclair Lewis published a book called *Main Street.* In it he drew a stinging picture of the narrow life and snobbishness in a town named Gopher Prairie. Lewis had grown up in Sauk Centre. No one doubted it was the model he used. But to Americans in the 1920s, *Main Street* spoke of more than one place. It attacked ignorance, prejudice, and shallowness that Lewis thought he saw in small-town people

The citizens of Sauk Centre were angered at first by Sinclair Lewis's bitter portrait of them. But slowly they forgave him. Fifty years later signs proudly told visitors that this was "The Original Main Street."

everywhere. Some read in it criticism of all American life. This fit in with the disappointed, bitter mood of the country after World War I. The book became a best-seller, and Sinclair Lewis became the state's most famous author.

For the next half-century Gopher Prairie was probably the best-known town in Minnesota. Then came Lake Wobegon. In the 1970s Garrison Keillor began hosting a radio show called "A Prairie Home Companion." He told stories about "the little town that time forgot." By 1985 so many people were listening and laughing that when he wrote the book *Lake Wobegon Days,* everyone knew it would sell.

If you could find them on a map, Lake Wobegon and Gopher Prairie would not be far apart. The main street, the water tower, and the grain elevator would look about the same. The people, too, are not a lot different. Most of them have lived near the town all their lives and like it. They stick to their own ways and are not curious about the rest of the world. But Keillor and Minnesotans who chuckle with him at the folks in Lake Wobegon have come a long way from Gopher Prairie in the 1920s.

Whether they choose to or not, many now live in cities. Long ago they or their parents said goodbye to places like Gopher Prairie and Lake Wobegon. Sometimes they wish they could go back. Even those who still live in small towns know that things have changed. The world has come a lot closer. They can laugh and say to themselves: "Yeah, that's how it used to be—and it wasn't so bad, either."

Sinclair Lewis

Garrison Keillor

What Makes Minnesota Different?

By the 1980s many Americans who had hardly heard of Minnesota knew all about Lake Wobegon. What image did they see? If they stopped to think about it, the name itself was a sly joke. It seemed like an Indian name, but when they said it aloud, they heard woe-be-gone—meaning to look sad and out of luck.

Some people say that this very kind of joke is part of the Minnesota image. In the 1970s cartoonist Richard Guindon made a hit with pictures of sober, sad-sack Minnesotans finding odd ways to cope with long blizzards and short heat waves. The weather is always worse in Minnesota. Boosters may brag about winter sports and 10,000 lakes. But most Minnesotans brag about surviving the cold and the mosquitoes. In 1983 librarians at the Minnesota Historical Society put together a list of jokes they heard. Some were:

Jack Frost loves Minnesota. He spends half his life here.

Have you jump-started your kid today?

Save a Minnesotan—eat a mosquito.

Entering Minnesota: Closed for glacier repairs, use alternate route.

Survive Minnesota and the rest of the world is easy.

Why Minnesota? To separate Ontario from Iowa.

The cartoons on these pages are by Richard Guindon.

"How's this? Rustic cabins, private beach, good walleye fishing . . ."

The worse the climate, the stronger people have to be. So the flip side of such jokes builds up another part of Minnesota's image—tough independence. Minnesota's independent politics are well known. No one was surprised when it was the only one of 50 states not to vote for Ronald Reagan as president in 1984. Its main political parties are not just Democrat and Republican, but Democratic-Farmer-Labor (DFL) and Independent Republican (IR).

Independence can take other forms, too. It can mean being your own boss, sticking to the family farm, starting a new business, inventing something, writing a book, organizing a labor union, or forming a cooperative. It means doing your own thing. People in the state are proud of Minnesotans like Bob Asp, who built the *Hjemkomst,* or Gary Spiess, who crossed the Atlantic alone in a 16-foot boat. They admire Will Steger and Ann Bancroft, who went to the North Pole by dogsled, and David Koontz, who walked around the world to help international understanding.

Some connect independence with what they hope will be Minnesota's future in new industries and high technology. In 1973 *Time* magazine predicted such a future and praised what it called Minnesota's "quality of life." Since then Minnesotans have tried hard to figure out just what this quality is. Writer and teacher Karal Ann Marling thinks it has something to do with balance and moderation. She sees Minnesota as a land "of fish and old-time things, of losers and stars, of lakes and modest skyscrapers." She also thinks the struggle to find its own image is part of what the state is all about. Maybe that is because there are so many different Minnesotas.

"Don't I know you?"

AUGUST 13, 1973

TIME

The Good Life In Minnesota

Gov. Wendell Anderson

Index

Page numbers in italics indicate illustrations.

Illustration Credits

All images reproduced in this book that are not listed here or identified as to source are owned by the Minnesota Historical Society. The names of artists are omitted here when they have been included in captions. Photographers are listed when known.

Cover: Fort Snelling painting by Edward K. Thomas, The Minneapolis Institute of Arts.

Table of Contents: Unit I Photo by Stephen Sandell. Unit II Printed by permission of the National Map Collection, Public Archives of Canada (C-35062). Unit V Library of Congress. Unit VI Minnesota Tourism Division.

Chapter 1: 10 Photo by Thomas Bremer. 12 Map by Rhoda Gilman. 13, 14 Photos by Margaret A. Ontl, *Red Wing Republican Eagle.* 15 Drawing by L. E. Blessing, *Minnesota Archaeologist;* photo courtesy Goodhue County Historical Society. 17 Map by Patricia Isaacs. 20 Photo courtesy of Jean M. Chesley.

Chapter 2: 22 Photo by Thomas Bremer. 24 Map by Patricia Isaacs. 25 Train photo by W. H. Illingworth; Hawley photo by Thomas Bremer. 26 Drawing by Orabelle Thortvedt. 28 Photo by S. P. Wange, courtesy of Robert A. Brekken. 29 Hawley photo by Thomas Bremer. 30, 31 Photos by Thomas Bremer. 32 Top photo by Roger Asp; bottom photo by Greg Asp. 33 *Hjemkomst* photo by Tom Asp.

Chapter 3: 34 Photo by Thomas Bremer. 36 Diagram by Rhoda Gilman. 38 Photo courtesy Hibbing Historical Society. 39 Power photo courtesy Hibbing Historical Society. 43 Photos by Thomas Bremer.

Chapter 4: 44 Photo by Thomas Bremer. 46 Photo by Thomas Bremer; map by Patricia Isaacs. 48 Etching by George Resler; photo by James Taylor Dunn. 50 Currie photo, *St. Paul Pioneer Press Dispatch.* 52, 53 Photos, *St. Paul Pioneer Press Dispatch.*

Chapter 5: 54 Drawing by Lee Radzak. 56 Drawings from *Memoirs,* American Anthropological Association; map by Patricia Isaacs. 57 Drawing by Lee Radzak. 58 Knife drawing by Karen Mattison, *Minnesota Archaeologist;* petroglyph drawing by Gordon A. Lothson; photo by Michael Budak. 59 Pot drawing from *Minnesota Archaeologist;* Woodland drawing by Lee Radzak. 60 Photo courtesy The Science Museum of Minnesota. 61 Drawing by Ann Tristani.

Chapter 6: 62 Watercolor by Seth Eastman. 64 From sketch by Frank B. Mayer courtesy Rare Books and Manuscripts Division, The New York Public Library, Astor, Lenox and Tilden Foundations; map by Patricia Isaacs. 65 Photo of Seth Eastman painting by Hillel Burger, Peabody Museum, Harvard University. 66 Watercolor by Seth Eastman from the collection of the James J. Hill Reference Library, St. Paul. 67 Painting by Frederic Remington, *Colliers.* 68, 69 Kettle and makuk drawings by David Christofferson from Robert C. Wheeler, *A Toast to the Fur Trade* (1985), courtesy Wheeler Productions, St. Paul. 68 Painting by Francis Lee Jacques courtesy Minnesota Arrowhead Association. 69 Watercolor by Seth Eastman from the collection of the James J. Hill Reference Library. 70 Painting by Seth Eastman. 71 Falls painting by Henry Lewis.

Chapter 7: 72 Painting by Francis Lee Jacques. 74 Stone ax drawing by Chester Kozlak; iron ax by Rhoda Gilman; map by Patricia Isaacs. 75 Drawing from Wheeler, *A Toast to the Fur Trade.* 76 Drawing by Rhoda Gilman; photo by Ellen B. Green. 77 Animal drawings by Rhoda Gilman; watercolor by Seth Eastman, from the collection of the James J. Hill Reference Library. 79 Map by Patricia Isaacs.

Chapter 8: 82, 83 Maps by Rhoda Gilman. 85 Catlin sketch, National Museum of American Art (formerly National Collection of Fine Arts), Smithsonian Institution, gift of Mrs. Joseph Harrison Jr. 87 Fort Snelling painting by Alfred Sully, The Thomas Gilcrease Institute of American History and Art. 89 Photo of Fort Snelling artifacts by Elizabeth Wehrwein. 89 Kane painting, Royal Ontario Museum. 91 Mayer sketch, Edward E. Ayer Collection, The Newberry Library.

Chapter 9: 92 Painting by S. Holmes Andrews. 95 Map by Rhoda Gilman. 97 Sketch by Robert O. Sweeny. 98 Cabin drawing by Rhoda Gilman from a photo in *Owatonna Centennial, 1854-1954.* 99 Painting by Thomas C. Healy. 102 Painting by Andrew Falkenshield. 104 Donnelly photo, National Archives.

Chapter 10: 106 Photo of Pyle painting by Gary Mortenson. 108 Lithograph by Edwin Whitefield. 110 Etchings from *Century Magazine.* 112 Photo courtesy of Elizabeth Bowler Morlock and Nancy Bowler Leebens.

Chapter 11: 114 Photo by Eric Mortenson of painting by Alexander Schwendinger, Brown County Historical Society. 116 Map by Rhoda Gilman. 118 Little Crow painting from watercolor by T. W. Wood. 120 Lincoln portrait from Clarence P. Hornung, *Handbook of Early Advertising Art;* Lincoln letter photo by Elizabeth Wehrwein; travois drawing by Robert O. Sweeny. 121 Painting by James G. McGrew.

Chapter 12: 124 Rossiter painting, University Art Museum, University of Minnesota, Minneapolis/gift of Daniel S. Feidt, 73.8.3. 126 Grain cradle from Willard W. Cochrane, *The Development of American Agriculture: A Historical Analysis,* copyright © 1979 by the University of Minnesota, reprinted with permission; "Plowing the Prairies Beyond the Mississippi," from *Harper's Weekly.* 129 Hay rake from John G. Wells, *The Grange Illustrated or Patron's Handbook;* grasshopper etching from *Frank Leslie's Illustrated Newspaper.* 131 Sulky plow from Cochrane, *The Development of American Agriculture.* 132 Breaking plow from *The Farmers Union.*

Chapter 13: 136 Map by Patricia Isaacs. 139 Map by Patricia Isaacs. 140 Cartoon from *St. Paul Pioneer Press;* photo from Flaten/Wange Collection, Clay County Historical Society. 141, 142 Logging photos by John Runk. 143 Train photo by William F. Roleff.

Chapter 14: 144 Painting from Luther College Collection, Vesterheim, Decorah, Iowa. 149 Newspaper office photo courtesy Nicollet County Historical Society. 154 Quarantine sign from Minnesota Department of Health.

Chapter 15: 160 Etching from *Harper's Weekly.* 162 Drawing courtesy Hibbing Historical Society. 164 Map by Patricia Isaacs. 165 Cartoon from *Minneapolis Journal.*

Chapter 16: 166 Painting from The Minneapolis Institute of Arts. 169 Photo courtesy St. Louis County Historical Society. 171 Streetcar sketch from *St. Paul Globe.* 175 Van Lear photo courtesy Hennepin County Historical Society.

Chapter 17: 178 Masterson portrait from *Soldiers of the Great War,* Vol. II (1920).

Chapter 18: 186 Advertisement from *The Radio Record.* 192 Photo, National Archives. 193 Emergency Conservation emblem from *Indians at Work;* map by Patricia Isaacs.

Chapter 19: 194 Photo by Shin Koyama, courtesy Hammel Green and Abrahamson, Inc. 197 Milking photo courtesy Stearns County Historical Society. 198 Photo courtesy Steiger Tractor, Inc. 199 Hawley photo by Thomas Bremer. 100 Map by Patricia Isaacs. 201 World Trade Center photo courtesy BCE Development Properties Inc.

Chapter 20: 204 Photo by Les Blacklock. 206 Photos from author's collection. 207 Medical center photo by Lee Snyder, courtesy St. Paul-Ramsey Medical Center. 209 Photo from *Star Tribune* (Mpls./St. Paul). 210 Photo by A. Vincent Scarano. 211 AIM leaders from Wide World Photos; Red School House photo by Wendy Gilbert. 212 Map by Patricia Isaacs. 213 Photos from *Star Tribune* (Mpls./St. Paul). 214 Taconite photo courtesy Reserve Mining Co.

Chapter 21: 216 Photo by Jack Flynn, Geographer. 218 Portrait by Eastman Johnson, courtesy St. Louis County Historical Society. 220 Statue photo by A. F. Raymond; falls photo by T. W. Ingersoll. 221 Gophers adapted from cartoon by Robert O. Sweeny; loons painting by Les C. Kouba. 223 Lewis portrait by Richard Hood; Keillor photo, *St. Paul Pioneer Press Dispatch.* 224, 225 Cartoons from *Guindon* (Minneapolis: Star & Tribune, 1977). 225 Cover © copyright 1973 Time Inc. All rights reserved. Reprinted by permission from TIME.

Other Credits

Chapter 3: 41 "North Country Blues" copyright 1963 WARNER BROS. INC. All rights reserved. Used by Permission.

Chapter 21: 218 Stanzas from "Red River Valley" quoted in *Alberta Historical Review,* Winter 1965.